PLENTIFUL
adjective

existing in or yielding
great quantities; abundant.

VEGAN JAMAICAN RECIPES TO REPEAT

PLENTIFUL

DENAI MOORE

Hardie Grant

BOOKS

FOOD THAT I DREAM ABOUT BEFORE GOING TO BED

SALADS THAT AREN'T LAME

ROMANTICISE COOKING FOR ONE

COMFORT GRUB

NUFF-BUFF
AND PLENTIFUL

My food journey began in my Jamaican childhood home with a garden full of fresh produce.

We had three different types of mango tree, a soursop tree, a cherry tree, an ackee tree, a tamarind tree and a coconut tree, plus generous neighbours, family and friends who grew a huge variety of other amazing ingredients. Being around such a bounty of fresh produce, accessible at my fingertips every day, made me value vegetables and fruits at their peak – eating seasonally is ingrained in me.

Jamaican food is often misrepresented, stripped of its complexity and reduced to being a meat-heavy cuisine. I want to debunk this myth about Jamaican food – I want to show you how exciting, diverse and vibrant vegan Jamaican flavours truly are. The use of spices in Jamaica is so unique, it's a melting pot of different cultures coming together.

Making food is an act of self-love for me. I've always loved cooking, but I really discovered myself in the kitchen when I stopped eating meat and dairy in 2016. I thought I might miss out on all the food I grew up eating after going vegan, but it just brought me closer to my childhood plate. I began to put together the flavours of my youth with all the ideas I had in my head, and cooking became an obsession.

However, music was my first love. When I was given an acoustic guitar at the age of 11 by my primary school music teacher, it was only a matter of time before I started writing sad songs. I remember watching Lauryn Hill's MTV Unplugged and feeling so

OUR FOOD CULTURES AND THE PASSING DOWN OF RECIPES FROM GENERATION TO GENERATION MAKE THE WORLD A BETTER PLACE.

seen. I knew then that I could be whatever artist I wanted to be. (Unfortunately, one of the first songs I learned how to play was 'Wonderwall' by Oasis. I think all my 'Wonderwall' slander over the years has deeply offended the rock gods and cursed me.) I started touring professionally when I was just a fresh faced 19-year-old, and it was this that expanded my food knowledge. I remember going from city to city, eating the most incredible food. I would create imaginary restaurant menus in notebooks (some of which I still have) and it made me want to create my own recipes and share them with people. I would invite my friends over for impromptu dinners, where even I didn't know what I was going to make. Would it be three or five courses? Would there be freshly churned ice cream? WHO knew?! That's the place that I enjoy cooking from the most, when I can let my childlike imagination run free and explore!

When I finally had the guts to cook for strangers and host my first ever supper club on 28 October 2017, I knew instantly that I was always meant to cook for others. I can't think of a better way to introduce myself than with a plate of food that I've made. It's my favourite way to say hello to 35+ new people. I thrive on toeing that line between my comfort zone and what's beyond. I love that when you try something new, it can be a revelation, or a bad idea, or a reason to try again. Dee's Table lived on beyond that supper club through to restaurant residencies and various London markets, where some of the dishes in this book were born, like the plantain gnocchi (then titled 'Rasta Pasta'), which I had made first for a friend and then debuted at a weekend-long residency at Buster Mantis in Deptford, London.

It's not unusual to fear what you might miss out on when going vegan. But when you unpack what it is that makes a delicious plate of food, you come to understand that eating vegan is not a hindrance at all. Making something delicious doesn't depend on animal products. There are so many natural sources of pure umami flavour – salty seaweed, rich and caramelised sticky onions, molasses, woody dried mushrooms. I find myself craving heat, deeply savoury flavours and texture – crispy! creamy! tangy! rich! Also, delicious doesn't mean complicated. I love simple flavours and classic combinations. They are there for a reason, because they've been tried and tested, eaten time and time again, enjoyed by many taste buds. They are the foundation that grounds us. Freshly baked bread with butter is still unbeatable! Garlic and onions fried in hot oil are the best! Mac and cheese, the ultimate comfort!

Food memories and traditions are so important, too. Our food cultures and the passing down of recipes from generation to generation make the world a better place. My grandma's porridge recipe will be forever a part of my history, memories of it brought back to me whenever I get a whiff of freshly grated nutmeg. For me, food is an extension of joy. I love a romantic solo meal, in which I'm both the main character and the supporting actress. I live for long, floaty dinner parties that make time feel like an illusion, everything stopping for a moment. Or just a quick weeknight pasta and wine catch-up session with good company. I could go on.

I could talk about food forever.
I think food and music play such
a key part in our lives – they are our
personal DNA, and they go hand
in hand. I can go back to a specific
place from just the smell of the
ocean and the lingering scent
of fried festival.

At heart, I'm just a massive self-
proclaimed foodie – you'll find me
at the hot new farmers' market in
town, buying up all the homemade
kimchi and seasonal ingredients or
at the newest ramen spot, gushing
over a shroomy broth and hand-
pulled noodles (because NOODLES
ARE EVERYTHING?!). I believe in
eating well, trying new things and
being present with the food in front
of you. I won't hesitate to book
a table for myself for dinner.
I will always savour every bite.

These recipes are my very own
creations – they were each born from
the idea or memory of something
I missed or craved, and then
I recreated that memory in a new
way, without recipes, just from my
intuition. There are no limitations
in food – it's about engaging with
a feeling and cooking with no rules.

BEFORE YOU ENTER INTO THE WORLD OF PLENTIFUL

You may notice that this book is organised in a very particular way. The chapters are specific to the way I think about food, how I CRAVE and celebrate food, on my own and with the people I love. So, for example, there is a chapter of recipes specifically designed for making just for yourself (see pages 62–83), as well as for special occasions (see pages 102–21) and when you're cooking for friends (see pages 122–45).

While this book doesn't include all the greatest Jamaican hits (please don't come for me!), I tried my best to remain sincere to my favourite things about Jamaican food. Honouring the vastness, honouring the depth (its roots are deep!) and sharing recipes for those dishes that mean the most to me. Also, although this book includes a lot of nostalgia from my childhood, I would be nothing without the flavours, techniques and vibrancy of East and Southeast Asian cuisine. To me, food from these regions is still massively devalued when you think about the impact it has had in the culinary world. It's the baseline of so many cooking techniques and methods for creating well-rounded dishes. There are many recipes inspired by East and Southeast Asian dishes in my book, such as my larb (see page 68) for one, or brown stew ramen (see page 98). They are not traditional in the slightest, but were born out of my sheer appreciation for the food I love to eat outside of my own culture. Life without it would be utterly tragic. (Thank you, thank you, thank you, thank you, thank you!)

I wrote this book because I'll simply never stop being curious about food. I'm a proud novice who wants to explore.

I wrote this book because I fantasise about hosting dinner parties that everyone raves about for weeks afterwards (yes, weeks, it's my fantasy).

I wrote this book because I wanted to trick everyone into reading my foodie hot takes.

I wrote this book to be cooked from through all the seasons (so leave it in an accessible nook in the kitchen, on hand from summer to winter and all the in-between parts).

I wrote this book to help you create a new obsession with your local Asian supermarket and greengrocers.

I wrote this book to fund and fast track my 'Kelis Farm' era.

I wrote this book to share! Please gift it to a friend, photograph the recipe you're most excited about, make it and repeat.

I hope that in eating my food you are somehow transported to a memory, that making these dishes provides a sense of familiarity in a different context. I hope that I can show you how to use an ingredient in a new way or help you to practise romance with yourself by dining with flowers and candles. Most of all, that you share lots of lols and funny moments over Frozen Lychee Margs (see page 143)!

So, as you enter the world of *Plentiful*, please linger. Earmark your favourite pages. She's yours to have now.

THINGS THAT MAKE ME THINK OF JAMAICA

Warm toasty spices filled with nostalgia. Thyme, spring onions (scallions), scotch bonnet, allspice. The simplicity of a freshly cut sweet jelly (green) coconut. Saturday soup with lots and lots of spinners. Roasted and fried breadfruit. My mum's fried dumplings. Callaloo with lots of garlic and onions. A freshly baked flaky patty (or two). Nutmeg-scented polenta (cornmeal) porridge. Captain's hard dough bread. A really good festival by the beach. Hard food with a little bit of curry or brown stew gravy. Hard food with some vegan butter ... Well, hard food in general. Plantain (pronounced 'plantin' – yes, I said what I said). Sorrel on Christmas Eve. My grandma's Hominy Corn Porridge (see page 39). Stew peas and fluffy white rice with a touch of really good hot sauce. An ice-cold ginger beer. FRESH ackee. Rundown. Rice and peas. Sun-ripe mangoes, my favourite fruit. Soft, charred roti.

MY PANTRY

Having a well-stocked pantry is essential for unlocking bold flavours. I can be a little bit of a pantry food hoarder – I'm guilty of going into an Asian supermarket and buying all the dried mushrooms and seaweed.

You don't need any spells or expensive superfoods to make delicious vegan food, but understanding what each ingredient can provide to a dish is key, whether that's rich umami depth, freshness from a pickle, a sweet edge or a spicy kick. Let your pantry become your playground – choose different elements to create a perfectly imperfect balancing act.

Here are the essentials in my kitchen.

 ## UMAMI

TOMATO

Tomatoes are one of the best natural sources of both acidity and sweetness. When roasted or dried they take on more salty notes, adding an umami flavour to sauces and dressings or becoming an unexpected pop of flavour in a rich, creamy dish like mac and cheese.

Tomato purée (paste)
Sun-dried tomatoes
Roasted tomatoes

SEAWEED

While extremely nutritious and rich in vitamins, seaweed is also a great ingredient for capturing those deep, salty flavours. A sheet of kombu in your soup instantly gives the dish a more rounded flavour.

Vegan dashi powder
Nori sheets
Kombu
Wakame

DRIED MUSHROOMS

One of my all-time favourite ingredients. You can blend dried mushrooms to add to your favourite dried seasoning to add an extra 'meaty' note, or throw a handful in any dish that requires a long cooking time, such as a stew.

Shiitake
Porcini
Cloud ear mushrooms
Mixed wild mushrooms
Smoked oyster mushrooms

FRESH MUSHROOMS

Although they're not as potent as in their dried form, fresh mushrooms add a more subtle meaty flavour and texture to any dish that would normally have beef or chicken in it. They also hold on to sauces well and will absorb any gravy and delicious juices.

Enoki mushrooms
Oyster mushrooms
Portobello mushrooms
Shimeji mushrooms
Chestnut (cremini) mushrooms
Maitake (hen of the woods) mushrooms

●● STORE CUPBOARD ESSENTIALS

OILS

I always like to keep these types of oil on hand. Coconut oil is a great replacement for vegetable shortening or butter and for using in baked goods. Extra virgin olive oil and avocado oil are good for dressings and finishing dishes. Avocado or vegetable oil are great neutral oils that have a high smoke point, so they are perfect for frying and sautéing vegetables.

Coconut oil
Extra virgin olive oil
Avocado oil
Vegetable oil

NUT AND SEED BUTTERS

Nut and seed butters have several amazing uses. They're great for finishing and topping dishes and for baking, and I love to use them in savoury dishes to make dressings and sauces.

I particularly love using tahini in sweet and savoury dishes – it's got a bitterness and richness that works so well in dressings for salads or on toast with mango lemon curd. Almond butter and peanut butter also work really well in desserts and in savoury dips.

Tahini
Almond butter
Peanut butter
Cashew butter

SUGARS AND SWEETENERS

Growing up in Jamaica, I only ever had unrefined brown sugar. It has so much more flavour and texture than white sugar. Another complex sweetener is date nectar, which is perfect for balancing a dressing.

I love using coconut sugar in savoury dishes like brown stew (see page 98), as it is subtle and has savoury notes. Agave is amazing for ice cream, as it freezes really well, reducing the possibility of ice crystals. Essentially just burnt cane sugar, black treacle (molasses) is the sweet equivalent of caramelised onions. In fact, it is great in very small doses when browning onions or garlic in oil.

These sources of sweetness are pretty much interchangeable based on what is available to you.

Dark brown sugar
Light brown sugar
Date nectar or syrup
Coconut sugar
Agave syrup
Black treacle (molasses)

ACID

The easiest way to add vibrancy to a dish is by using fresh lemon or lime juice, or different types of vinegar. A splash of acid is always a great finisher before serving a dish.

Limes
Lemons
Oranges

Grapefruit
Apple cider vinegar
White wine vinegar

SALT

Good salt is so important. When it's good, you don't really need that much of it. I always season in different stages with different forms of salt, like adding a splash of tamari or soy sauce to a dish. Salt is also very important for sweet dishes. I use fine sea salt in pretty much all of my desserts, and a pinch of flaky sea salt is amazing for finishing a gooey cookie.

Flaky sea salt
Fine sea salt
Smoked sea salt
Soy sauce and tamari

SPICES AND DRIED HERBS

These are the spices and dried herbs that filled my Jamaican household with scent. Allspice (also called pimento) is essential and can be used in so many different ways, it's amazing for dry rubs and an important part of jerk, which is traditionally cooked over pimento wood. Freshly grated nutmeg is such a different thing from the ground dried stuff. It is much more fragrant and is used in both savoury and sweet dishes. Smoked paprika, although it isn't a very traditional Jamaican spice, is really amazing for vegan cooking. It adds a lovely smoky hit to any dish. A fresh green seasoning is an essential in my kitchen, to be used as the base for many dishes.

Allspice berries
Ground allspice
Whole nutmeg
Vanilla pods (beans) and extract
Smoked paprika
Garlic granules
Onion powder
Cinnamon sticks
Bay leaves

Dried thyme
Coriander seeds
Curry powder
Ground turmeric
Green Seasoning (see page 208)

TINNED FOODS

Although I love cooking pulses from their dried state, having cooked, tinned pulses on hand allows for stress-free and quick cooking. I love to use jackfruit as a meat replacement and in stews, while coconut milk is essential in Jamaican cooking, from rundown and rice and peas to hominy corn porridge. Always look for a tin with the least ingredients and a high percentage of coconut cream. I use the heart of the palm as an amazing stand in for fish (see page 37).

Pulses (legumes) such as kidney beans, cannellini beans, chickpeas, butter (lima) beans, green and brown lentils

Green jackfruit
Coconut milk
Heart of palm

GRAINS

I grew up eating mainly white rice but made the transition to eating more of a variety of grains when going vegan. There are so many earthy flavours that aren't present in white rice.

Brown and white rice
Quinoa
Buckwheat
Coarse polenta (cornmeal)

FLOUR

Different flours are best suited to different dishes. When it comes to fried dumplings, self-raising (self-rising) is the best, but I love using spelt for baked treats or pancakes and gram (chickpea) flour is great for gluten-free recipes.

Spelt flour
Wholemeal (whole-wheat) flour
Unbleached white flour
Almond flour
Gram (chickpea) flour
Self-raising (self-rising) flour

▶▶▶ FRESH AND CHILLED INGREDIENTS

FRESH SEASONAL PRODUCE

I'm a strong advocate for buying local, seasonal produce. It's so important to go and support your farmers' market, and possibly try something new. The key ingredients in a lot of the recipes in this book are completely interchangeable for vegetables that are readily available of a similar texture. Week to week, I always have seasonal dark greens, a range of cruciferous vegetables from the cabbage family, a starchy carbohydrate like potatoes, and mushrooms.

Dark leafy greens (spinach, kale, etc.)
Chayote (also called cho cho)
Plantains
Pumpkins
Sweet potatoes
Carrots
Broccoli
Avocadoes

Potatoes
Peppers
Cabbage
Aubergines (eggplants)
Spring onions (scallions)
Mangoes
Pineapples
Passion fruit
Pears

NON-DAIRY MILK

Deciding what type of milk to use in a dish is down to preference and what you want to achieve in the overall flavour and consistency. For baking, soya milk works perfectly in my opinion, as it's higher in protein and is closer to dairy milk. I love to cook with coconut milk as it's so creamy and adds a lot of richness to both savoury and sweet dishes.

Soya milk
Coconut milk

FRESH HERBS

Thyme is my favourite herb of all time and is the soy sauce of Jamaican food. Chives achieve fresh notes of sweet onion, similar to spring onions (scallions). I love to finish dishes with them. I've really grown into loving fresh mint, it works so well in both savoury and sweet dishes and adds a wonderful vibrancy.

Thyme
Parsley
Chives
Coriander (cilantro)
Mint

VEGAN PROTEIN

I adore tofu because it is such an amazing vehicle for flavour, while silken tofu is amazing in desserts and sauces, adding a creamy, rich flavour. I don't usually eat meat replacements daily, however when recreating a particularly meaty dish, I utilise all the wonderful options that are now available.

Firm tofu
Silken tofu
Smoked tofu
Tempeh

FATS AND VEGAN CHEESE

Good vegan butter is so hard to come by. I usually go for Violife as an affordable and reliable option. Making vegan butter from scratch is a fulfilling process and surprisingly easy to do, too. I love using vegan cream cheese in icing (frosting) as it makes it lighter than the traditional all-butter icing.

Vegan block butter
Vegan spread
Vegan cream cheese
Vegan Cheddar

FERMENTED AND PICKLED INGREDIENTS

I'm pretty much obsessed with the ancient process of fermentation. Miso is one of my favourite cooking ingredients – a teaspoon of it in any savoury or 'meaty' dish really helps it pack a punch. It brings a rich, salty, umami depth. Coconut yoghurt is delicious and a great base for a sauce or dressing.

Miso
Pickled vegetables, such as red onions, gherkins (dill pickles), escovitch

Non-dairy yoghurt
Kimchi

THE KITCHEN EQUIPMENT I CAN'T LIVE WITHOUT

Having the right kitchen tools helps to make everyday cooking so easy and efficient. In the past I've been very impulsive and bought kitchen appliances that I hardly ever used. These are the tools I used throughout writing this book.

MICROPLANE GRATER

Owning a Microplane changed my life. I used mine for most of the recipes in the book. Great for grating garlic and citrus zest, they're also perfect for grating nutmeg, which is my favourite spice to smell as I'm using it.

HIGH-SPEED BLENDER

A high-speed blender is so, so handy and saves a lot of time. I use it for dressings and sauces, and I used it heavily in the baking section of the book. I really stand by my Vitamix, which I've had for over seven years now. The longest relationship I've managed to sustain.

FOOD PROCESSOR

Food processors are wonderful appliances that allow you to make many things simply and efficiently. Their cold metal blades also eliminate any heat that would otherwise come from your hands when making pastry.

A SMALL RUBBER SPATULA AND A BIG AND STURDY RUBBER SPATULA

I use my tiny spatula every day. It's so good for scraping down bowls and mixing things in small quantities. The big and sturdy spatulas are perfect for folding things in together – I use them for cake batters.

BAKING TRAYS (PANS)

You can never have enough of them! For vegan cooking these are a big-time essential. I'm a big believer in giving veg a lot of surface area when cooking, to allow them to crisp up through direct heat contact. By utilising a few different techniques you can make amazing food with only a baking tray.

LOAF TIN (PAN)

Half of the baked treats in this book are in loaf tins. I LOVE a loaf cake. I have various types, including a glass one and several non-stick stainless steel ones.

SPICE GRINDER AND PESTLE AND MORTAR

Freshly ground spices are so much more fragrant and powerful. I got a spice grinder as a birthday gift and it's honestly one of the best things that I own. I also like to break down herbs and pastes in a pestle and mortar. The experience feels quite meditative to me. I love anything that forces you to take your time.

WOODEN SPOON, METAL BALLOON WHISK, OFFSET SPATULA

I use these tools daily. Metal whisks are the most effective – I wouldn't recommend buying a plastic or silicone one. Offset spatulas are great for releasing cakes from tins (pans).

FOOD THAT I DREAM ABOUT BEFORE

G✳ING TO BED

I always dream about breakfast the night before. Like clockwork. The night-time is simply designed for food dreaming.

On Friday nights I'll be thinking about a late, hazy weekend breakfast. Something that might take a little longer to make, but as the process is accompanied by good coffee and Elliott Smith, it's always worth it.

On weekdays I dream about things on toast. I love roasted grapes and a smear of herby vegan cream cheese on a spring day, or tomatoes with whipped tofu in summer (see page 28). If I'm particularly hungry, I like to do a dessert piece of toast and a savoury one. A two-course meal for breakfast, if you like.

In the colder months I fantasise about warm, hearty bowls – both savoury and sweet. Maybe oats with a seasonal fruit compote and crunchy seeds, creamy Hominy Corn Porridge (see page 39) or some garlic and spring onion (scallion) mushrooms with a lick of cashew, nori and Scotch bonnet oil. Yum!

These are the recipes that keep me up at night from the sheer excitement of eating them the next day. Sleep is merely the interlude to my favourite meal of the day – breakfast!

HARD DOUGH FRENCH TOAST WITH WHIPPED ROASTED BANANA ALMOND BUTTER

SERVES 4   PREP TIME : 10 MINUTES   COOK TIME : 20 MINUTES

French toast is criminally underrated in my humble opinion. It's almost like a little personal serving of bread pudding with sweet toppings, which is a wonderful thing. When I have French toast, I always think, 'Why don't I make this more often?' This recipe is all about the whipped roasted banana almond butter. It's insanely delicious and you'll want to eat it straight from the bowl. Hard dough bread is the perfect sub for brioche – it's already slightly sweet and is very dense, which creates a pillowy texture.

FOOD THAT I DREAM ABOUT BEFORE GOING TO BED

400 ml (13 fl oz/generous 1½ cups) coconut milk

1 tablespoon chia seeds

1½ tablespoons cornflour (cornstarch)

1 tablespoon nutritional yeast

1 teaspoon vanilla extract

1 teaspoon ground cinnamon

1 tablespoon brown sugar

¼ teaspoon salt

freshly grated nutmeg, to taste

4 thick slices of hard dough bread

1 tablespoon vegan block butter

FOR THE WHIPPED ROASTED BANANA ALMOND BUTTER

1½ tablespoons vegan block butter

2 ripe bananas, sliced

1 teaspoon ground cinnamon

3 tablespoons maple syrup

50 ml (1¾ fl oz/3 tablespoons) dark rum

70 g (2¼ oz) almond butter

150 g (5 oz) vegan cream cheese

FOR THE CARAMELISED BANANAS

1 tablespoon vegan block butter

2 ripe bananas, halved lengthways

2 tablespoons maple syrup, plus extra to serve

First, make a custard. Combine all the ingredients for the French toast except the bread and butter in a shallow dish and whisk to combine.

Next, make the whipped roasted banana almond butter. In a frying pan (skillet), melt the butter over a medium heat. Once foamy and lightly browned, add the sliced bananas. Caramelise for 3–4 minutes, then add the cinnamon, maple syrup and rum. Flambé by tipping the pan into the flame on the hob (stovetop) or using a lighter. Cook for another 2–3 minutes to reduce. Transfer to a food processor with the almond butter and cream cheese. Blend until light and airy, then transfer to a bowl and set aside.

In the same pan, melt the butter for the caramelised bananas over a medium heat. Once foamy and lightly browned, add the bananas flat side down. Caramelise for 3–4 minutes, then add the maple syrup. Flip the bananas over and cook the other side. Set aside on a plate.

Heat the remaining butter in a frying pan over a medium heat. Dip the slices of bread, two at a time, into the custard mix for 30 seconds. Allow any excess to drip off, then fry for 3–4 minutes on each side until lovely and golden brown. Repeat with the other slices of bread.

Place a slice of French toast on a plate, top with the caramelised bananas, then add a good dollop of the whipped roasted banana almond butter and finish with extra maple syrup.

HARD DOUGH CHERRY BOSTOCK

SERVES 4   PREP TIME : 10 MINUTES   COOK TIME : 25 MINUTES

This cherry bostock will make your friends and family feel like they're in a fancy bakery. Essentially, bostock is a slice of stale brioche topped with frangipane and jam, and it's very easy to put together. As this recipe has simple components, I urge you to buy a really good-quality jam that is loaded with cherry flavour.

FOOD THAT I DREAM ABOUT BEFORE GOING TO BED

4 slices of hard dough bread

50 g (2 oz/⅓ cup) good-quality cherry jam

50 g (2 oz/generous ½ cup) flaked (slivered) almonds

FOR THE FRANGIPANE

100 g (3½ oz) vegan block butter

70 g (2¼ oz/scant ⅓ cup) caster (superfine) sugar

80 ml (3 fl oz/⅓ cup) soya milk

1 teaspoon vanilla extract

zest of 1 lemon

150 g (5 oz/1½ cups) ground almonds (almond meal)

50 g (2 oz/scant ½ cup) plain (all-purpose) flour

1¼ teaspoons baking powder

pinch of salt

Preheat the oven to 170°C (375°F/gas 5) and line a baking sheet with baking parchment.

Start by making the frangipane. In a saucepan, brown the block butter over a medium heat for 4½ minutes. Transfer to a bowl and add the caster sugar, milk, vanilla extract and lemon zest. Whisk until combined. In a separate bowl, combine the ground almonds, plain flour, baking powder and salt. Whisk to combine. Then, fold the dry ingredients into the wet ingredients.

Spread out the slices of hard dough bread on the prepared baking sheet. Spread a generous tablespoon of cherry jam on each slice, then add two tablespoons of the frangipane mixture onto each piece of bread, gently spreading it over the jam with a palette knife (spatula).

Sprinkle the flaked almonds over the top, then bake in the oven for 15–20 minutes until golden brown. Serve immediately with coffee.

SPICY SLOW-ROASTED TOMATOES AND SHALLOTS ON TOAST WITH WHIPPED SILKEN TOFU

SERVES 2–3   PREP TIME : 10 MINUTES   COOK TIME : 25 MINUTES

There's something about tomatoes and jammy shallots on toast. When tomatoes and onions are roasted and slightly charred they become smoky and create a wonderful sticky texture. This serves a few, but it is also a very good solo breakfast for one. The tomatoes keep well in the fridge and work wonderfully in a grilled cheese sandwich the next day.

3 tablespoons olive oil

1 baby shallot, sliced into rings

¾ teaspoon coriander seeds, roughly ground

½ teaspoon chilli flakes

285 g (10 oz) cherry tomatoes, half kept whole and half halved

2 garlic cloves, very finely chopped

1 tablespoon chopped thyme leaves

2 tablespoons balsamic glaze

2–3 slices of bread of your choice

salt and freshly ground black pepper

FOR THE WHIPPED TOFU

175 g (6 oz) silken tofu

small handful of coriander (cilantro) leaves

small handful of flat-leaf parsley leaves

1 garlic clove (optional, if you like the heat of raw garlic)

juice of ½ lemon

Preheat the oven to 180°C (400°F/gas 6).

Put all the ingredients for the whipped tofu except the lemon juice in a high-speed blender. Blend until completely smooth, adding the lemon juice slowly until the desired texture is achieved. Transfer to a bowl and set aside. I like to put it in the refrigerator for a cold contrast to the hot jammy tomatoes.

Heat the olive oil in an ovenproof frying pan (skillet) or casserole dish (Dutch oven) over a medium heat and fry the shallots with a good pinch of salt until lightly browned and softened. As it's sizzling, add the ground coriander seeds and chilli flakes. Next, add the tomatoes, garlic and thyme. Season again with salt and pepper, then drizzle with the balsamic glaze. Transfer to the oven to roast for 15–20 minutes until beautifully charred and blistered.

Toast the bread and divide between plates, then top with some of the whipped tofu and a few tablespoons of the tomatoes. Serve immediately.

SPRING ONION AND CHEDDAR BISCUITS WITH KIMCHI TOFU SCRAMBLE AND GREENS

SERVES 6   PREP TIME : 30 MINUTES, PLUS 30 MINUTES RESTING TIME   COOK TIME : 20 MINUTES

As a Jamaican I grew up eating American-style biscuits. Nothing compares to a well-made, tender biscuit. They are dangerously buttery and salty. This recipe is bursting with savoury flavour. The biscuits use non-dairy yoghurt instead of buttermilk, offering a wonderful sharp flavour. This is a big brunch plate – it would be a perfect holiday or celebration breakfast if you're cooking for your non-vegan family and want to quietly impress them.

FOR THE BISCUITS

250 g (9 oz/2 cups) plain (all-purpose) flour, plus extra for dusting

50 g (2 oz/⅓ cup) coarse polenta (cornmeal)

1 ½ tablespoons caster (superfine) sugar

1 teaspoon salt

1½ teaspoons baking powder

½ teaspoon bicarbonate of soda (baking soda)

3 tablespoons nutritional yeast

½ teaspoon garlic granules

1½ teaspoons freshly ground black pepper

50 g (2 oz) vegan Cheddar, grated

100 g (3½ oz) vegan block butter, frozen for 10 minutes then grated

4 spring onions (scallions), finely chopped

100 g (3½ oz) unsweetened soya yoghurt

2 tablespoons non-dairy milk of your choice, plus extra for brushing

FOR THE KIMCHI TOFU SCRAMBLE

1 tablespoon vegan block butter

1 tablespoon olive oil

1 red (bell) pepper, diced

1 spring onion (scallion), finely chopped

1 teaspoon ground turmeric

1 teaspoon garlic granules

300 g (10½ oz) silken tofu

50 g (2 oz) vegan-friendly kimchi, roughly chopped

1 teaspoon black salt (optional)

1 tablespoon nutritional yeast

splash of soya milk

salt and freshly ground black pepper

your favourite hot sauce, to serve

FOR THE GREENS

1 tablespoon vegan block butter

1 garlic clove, finely chopped

200 g (7 oz) spinach, sliced

200 g (7 oz) kale, sliced

splash of water

lemon juice, to taste

In a large bowl, combine the flour, polenta, sugar, salt, baking powder, bicarbonate of soda, nutritional yeast, garlic granules and pepper, whisking thoroughly to combine.

Mix the grated cheese and butter into the dry ingredients, gently rubbing in with your fingertips but making sure you leave little clumps. Now add the spring onions and stir to combine.

In a jug (pitcher), mix together the soya yoghurt and milk, then stir into the dry ingredients. Make sure you don't overmix. Transfer the dough to a very lightly floured surface and shape into a square (1). Cut in half (2), then stack together (3) and roll out again. Repeat. Wrap in cling film (plastic wrap) and rest in the refrigerator for at least 30 minutes.

Preheat the oven to 170°C (375°F/gas 5).

Roll out the biscuit dough into a 20 x 10 cm (8 x 4 inch) rectangle shape and use a sharp knife to cut into 6–8 square biscuits (4). Brush with a little milk, then bake in the oven for 15–20 minutes. As they're baking, make the tofu scramble and greens.

For the tofu scramble, heat the butter and olive oil in a frying pan (skillet) over a medium heat. Add the red pepper and spring onion and fry with a pinch of salt for 3–4 minutes until softened. Next, add the turmeric and garlic granules and fry for a further minute. Now add the block of silken tofu and the kimchi. Break it up in the pan with the back of a wooden spoon. Fry for 2 minutes, then add the nutritional yeast and a splash of milk. Season with salt and pepper to taste.

For the greens, heat the butter in a frying pan over a medium heat and fry the garlic until fragrant. Add the greens and a splash of water, cover with a lid and steam for 3–4 minutes until just cooked. Add a squeeze of lemon juice and salt and pepper to taste.

Serve the warm biscuits with the tofu and greens. Top with your favourite hot sauce and enjoy.

PICK-UP 'SALT FISH' AND PRESSED GREEN PLANTAIN

SERVES 4   PREP TIME::15 MINUTES   COOK TIME:7 MINUTES

As I was growing up, my mother would always make this on a weekend.
I'm normally a hardcore sweet plantain person, but when I get the craving for
it, fried green plantain really hits the spot. There's something about the raw,
almost ceviche-like texture of the heart of palm with the hot, crispy and salty
plantain. The recipe is very simple but so insanely delicious. The pick-up
'salt fish' is even better the second day, too!

1 small red onion, finely sliced

220 g (7¾ oz) hearts of palm, rinsed, drained and sliced into half-moons

100 g (3½ oz) cherry tomatoes, quartered

1 garlic clove, very finely chopped

handful of flat-leaf parsley, roughly chopped, plus extra to serve

1 nori sheet

juice of 1 lemon

glug of olive oil

salt and freshly ground black pepper

1 avocado, sliced, to serve

FOR THE PRESSED GREEN PLANTAIN

2 green plantains

vegetable oil, for frying

flaky sea salt

Put the onion into a bowl and cover with cold water. Leave to sit while you prepare everything else.

In a separate bowl, combine the hearts of palm with the tomatoes, garlic, parsley, nori, lemon juice, olive oil and salt and pepper to taste. Drain and pat dry the onions and add to the mix. Taste and adjust the seasoning. Set aside.

Top and tail the green plantains and remove the peel by running a sharp knife along it and then peeling back to separate it from the flesh. Cut on the diagonal into 6–8 big chunks.

In a frying pan (skillet), heat enough vegetable oil to coat the bottom of the pan over a medium-high heat. Fry the plantain slices for 3–4 minutes, flipping to cook on both sides. Remove and drain briefly on paper towels, then transfer to a board and use a mug or bowl to flatten the pieces. Fry again for a further 2–3 minutes until crispy. Drain again on paper towels and hit immediately with some flaky sea salt.

Sprinkle the 'salt fish' with a little more parsley, then serve with the green plantain and avocado.

THE ULTIMATE JAMAICAN BREAKFAST

SERVES 4–6   PREP TIME : 20 MINUTES, PLUS 1 HOUR RESTING TIME   COOK TIME : 20 MINUTES

Fried dumplings remind me of Sunday mornings. That was fried dumpling time
for my mother, and waking up to that smell was heavenly. You wouldn't make this
full version on a weekly basis – often I would have the dumplings with steamed
cabbage and salt fish, or even sausages and spicy baked beans. The recipe
below is with all the bells and whistles. With ackee and salt fish being the national
dish of Jamaica, it would feel strange to not include a recipe for it. It feels like
a 'I'm trying to impress my partner's family' kind of moment, or 'it's Easter
and I've been put in charge of breakfast'.

FOR THE DUMPLINGS

400 g (14 oz) self-raising flour (or 4 cups all-purpose flour plus 3½ teaspoons baking powder)

1 tablespoons light brown soft sugar

1 teaspoon salt

1 tablespoon vegan block butter

200 ml (7 fl oz/scant 1 cup) water

vegetable oil, for frying

FOR THE ACKEE AND 'SALT FISH'

2–3 tablespoons olive oil

1 red onion, diced

1 tomato, diced

1 Scotch bonnet, deseeded and chopped

1 spring onion (scallion), chopped

2 garlic cloves, chopped

350 g (12 oz) kale

splash of water

4 sprigs of thyme, leaves chopped

210 g (7½ oz) hearts of palm, roughly chopped

1 tablespoon vegan fish sauce

splash of water

500 g (1 lb 2 oz) tin of ackee, rinsed and drained

salt and freshly ground black pepper

your favourite hot sauce, to serve

FOR THE GARLICKY GREENS

1 tablespoon vegan block butter

4 garlic cloves, finely chopped

350 g (12 oz) spinach

FOR THE FRIED PLANTAINS

2 ripe plantains, peeled and sliced diagonally into 8 pieces

olive or vegetable oil, for frying

First make the dumplings. Put the flour, sugar and salt (and baking powder if using all-purpose flour) into a bowl with the butter. Using your fingertips, rub the butter into the dry ingredients. Add the water to bring it together, then knead in the bowl until you have a smooth dough. Cover with cling film (plastic wrap) and leave to rest for 1 hour. This will allow the gluten to fully hydrate and give you the fluffiest dumplings. Once rested, separate the dough into eight pieces, then form into balls by rolling in your hands. Set back in the bowl.

Next prepare the ackee and 'salt fish'. Heat the olive oil in a frying pan (skillet) over a medium heat. Sweat the onion for 2–3 minutes with a pinch of salt until softened, then add the tomato, Scotch bonnet, spring onion, garlic and thyme. Fry for a few more minutes until wonderfully fragrant. Now add the heart of palm and season with the vegan fish sauce. Fry for another minute. Add a splash of water to the pan to deglaze and then reduce the heat to a simmer. Add the ackee, cover with a lid and steam for 5 minutes.

For the plantains, in a separate frying pan, heat enough oil to coat over a medium heat and fry the plantain slices for 3–4 minutes until golden, flipping to cook each side.

Now make the garlicky greens. Heat the butter in a frying pan and once melted fry the garlic until fragrant. Add the kale and a splash of water. Season with salt and pepper, cover and steam for 2 minutes. Next add the spinach, put the lid back on and cook until just wilted. Check for seasoning.

Heat 2.5 cm (1 inch) of oil in a deep-sided heavy-bottomed frying pan over a medium heat. Test the temperature by using a wooden spoon – if lots of bubbles appear around it immediately, it's ready to go. Fry the dumplings for 3–4 minutes – be careful, if they are browning too quickly, the temperature of the oil is too high.

Put a couple of fried dumplings, some plantains and garlicky greens on each plate. Finally, add the ackee and 'salt fish' in the middle. Serve with your favourite hot sauce and enjoy!

HOMINY CORN PORRIDGE

SERVES 4–6   PREP TIME : 5 MINUTES, PLUS OVERNIGHT SOAKING TIME
COOK TIME : 1 HOUR 20 MINUTES

Jamaican porridge is one of my favourite things in the world. From polenta
(cornmeal) porridge or green banana porridge to hominy corn, as soon as the
winter months come by, I make myself a bowl of Jamaican porridge and I feel
safe. Hominy corn porridge is my favourite. My grandma always made it for me
when she lived in Sheffield and the smell of it simply brings me back to her.
In many ways, this is a homage to her. Except for the vegan dairy replacements,
this recipe is very similar to how I remember her making it.

200 g (7 oz/generous 1 cup) dried
yellow hominy corn

1.5 litres (50 fl oz/6½ cups) water

generous pinch of salt

2 tablespoons coconut sugar or
brown sugar, plus extra to serve

2 cinnamon sticks

1 bay leaf

1 tablespoon vanilla extract

400 ml (13 fl oz/1½ cups) coconut milk

100 ml (3½ fl oz/scant ½ cup) soya milk

freshly grated nutmeg, to taste

condensed coconut milk, to sweeten

The day before, put the dried hominy into a bowl,
cover with cold water and leave to soak overnight.

The next day, drain and rinse the hominy and put it in
a saucepan with the water, salt and sugar. Bring to the
boil, then add the cinnamon sticks, bay leaf and vanilla
extract. Boil for 5 minutes then reduce the heat to a
simmer and cover with a lid. Cook for about 65 minutes,
stirring occasionally, until very soft.

Add the coconut milk and bring back to the boil, then boil
for 5 minutes. Transfer a third of the mixture to a high-
speed blender and blend until smotth. This is to thicken
the porridge. Add back to the porridge, along with the
soya milk. Simmer for 5 more minutes until thickened.

Grate a generous amount of nutmeg into the porridge
and sweeten to taste with condensed coconut milk,
coconut sugar or brown sugar. Serve in bowls with some
more grated nutmeg on top.

THE ULTIMATE
BREAKFAST PARATHA

SERVES 4   PREP TIME : 10 MINUTES   COOK TIME : 15 MINUTES

As a paratha stan, I simply had no choice in creating this recipe. I simply don't know what I did before my frozen paratha obsession began. Well, it's more like a lifestyle at this point. They are the perfect freezable food, just as good as fresh when fried, and so versatile. I've used them for desserts, as pitta-style chips ... the list goes on. Here, I've used them as a vessel for ackee and plantain. While writing this book, this was my weekend brekky after one too many frozen margs (see page 143) the night before. I've made them for friends that stayed the night and made paratha addicts out of them, too. This recipe includes a different twist on vegan ackee and 'salt fish', using artichokes. This dish is often served with fried dumplings or hard food, and the paratha offers a wonderful twist.

1 tablespoon olive oil, plus extra for frying the plantains

1 red onion, diced

1 tomato, diced

½ Scotch bonnet, deseeded and chopped

1 spring onion (scallion), chopped, plus extra to serve

2 garlic cloves, chopped

1 tablespoon chopped thyme leaves

350 g (12 oz) rinsed and drained ackee

200 g (7 oz) marinated artichokes, roughly chopped

splash of water

2 ripe plantains, peeled and sliced diagonally into 8 pieces

4 frozen paratha

FOR THE SPICY SWEET YOGHURT

4 tablespoons plain dairy-free yoghurt

1 tablespoon chilli jam

splash of your favourite hot sauce, to taste

Heat the olive oil in a frying pan (skillet) over a medium heat and add the onion with a pinch of salt and sweat for 2–3 minutes until softened. Add the tomato, Scotch bonnet, spring onion, garlic and thyme and fry for a couple of minutes until fragrant. Now add the artichokes and fry for a further minute. Add a splash of water to the pan to deglaze and then reduce to a simmer. Add the ackee, cover and steam for 5 minutes.

In a separate frying pan, heat enough oil to coat over a medium heat and fry the plantain slices for 3–4 minutes until golden, flipping to cook each side.

Mix together all the ingredients for the yoghurt in a small bowl.

Heat a dry frying pan over a medium heat and cook the paratha, one at a time, for 1–2 minutes on each side.

Place a paratha on a plate, add a dollop of the spicy yoghurt, some plantain and then the ackee mixture. Garnish with some more spring onions or hot sauce.

SALADS
THAT

AREN'T LAME

Salads have a bad rep for being boring and I just think we've been salad'ing the wrong way for years. For some reason I'm really haunted by the meme of the woman eating salad while happy. I feel like it's such an after thought for most people, when a good salad can be so satisfying. They should have something fresh! crunchy! zippy! creamy! vibrant! There's so much untapped potential beyond the peppery leaves with a little drizzle of balsamic vinegar and olive oil. Anything can go into a salad, so it's actually such an exciting thing to create. At home, I look into my cupboard and pick as I go. Maybe some sultanas (golden raisins), some seeds for crunch. Lots of herbs! It's also how I get rid of lots of veg that's on their last legs – I love a fridge raid salad moment! These salads are strong and sturdy and will have everyone fighting over them at the dinner table.

MELON AND CHO CHO SALAD

SERVES 4   PREP TIME : 5 MINUTES

In lockdown I got hooked on melon, and that's melon of all kinds. I'm not sure why, but as the supermarket was the event of the week, I took my time to walk around and got hooked in melon season. This is a salad to be eaten seasonally, as it uses so few ingredients, so it's important that each one has the best opportunity to shine. The melon could be cold and crisp if that's your vibe!

1 small cantaloupe, sliced

1 chayote (cho cho), finely sliced on a mandoline

1 shallot, sliced into half-moons

30 mint leaves

50 g (2 oz/⅓ cup) roasted and salted Marcona almonds

splash of coconut vinegar (or white wine vinegar)

glug of crème de la crème olive oil

salt and freshly ground black pepper

Combine all the ingredients in a large bowl and toss together. Plate up, then sprinkle with salt to taste.

MOBAY SOM TAM
WITH BURNT LIME DRESSING

SERVES 4   PREP TIME : 20 MINUTES   COOK TIME : 10 MINUTES

This salad is inspired by the amazing som tam salad from Thailand, which uses green papaya and is viciously spicy and heady with salty brightness. I wanted to use mangoes instead. Green mangos are perfect for this salad. Their tart and slightly firmer flesh gives more of a bite to the dish. The flavours in this salad are bold: nori, roasted salted peanuts, crispy shallots, burnt limes. All the best things. It is a salad that will surprise you by how punchy it is.

1 slightly unripe mango

1 carrot, julienned or finely sliced

bunch of coriander (cilantro), leaves picked

handful of mint leaves

handful of roasted and salted peanuts

2 tablespoons nori flakes

handful of crispy shallots

FOR THE DRESSING

1½ limes, halved

1 garlic clove, very finely chopped

2½ tablespoons palm sugar, coconut sugar or brown sugar

½ or ¼ Scotch bonnet, finely chopped

1 tablespoon vegan fish sauce

Start by preparing the mango. Using a vegetable peeler, remove the skin from the mango, then use a sharp knife to cut the flesh from the mango on all sides. Cut each part in half, then cut into thin strips. Put the strips into a bowl with the carrot and herbs.

Next make the dressing. If you have a gas hob (stovetop), use tongs to hold the limes over the flame, flesh side down, until charred. If you don't have a gas hob, heat a little oil in a frying pan (skillet) over a medium high heat and fry the limes flesh side down until charred.

In a bowl, combine the garlic, sugar, Scotch bonnet and vegan fish sauce, then squeeze in the juice of the burnt limes. Taste and adjust the flavours if necessary.

Add the dressing to the prepared vegetables and toss to coat. Add the peanuts, then transfer to a serving platter, garnishing with the nori flakes and crispy shallots just before serving.

ZIPPY GARLICKY CUCUMBER AND CHO CHO SALAD

SERVES 2–3   PREP TIME: 10 MINUTES

Cho cho, aka chayote is so insanely delicious raw, yet it's never prepared that way in Jamaican cooking! I love the sturdy crunch it offers, it really holds the dressing and works really well alongside the cuke, which is it's cooler cousin flavour-wise.

1 cucumber, finely sliced

1 chayote (cho cho), finely sliced

½ red onion, finely sliced

handful of flat-leaf parsley, roughly chopped

10 mint leaves, finely chopped

salt and freshly ground black pepper

FOR THE DRESSING

1 garlic clove, very finely chopped

½ Scotch bonnet, deseeded and very finely chopped

zest and juice of 1 lime

2 tablespoons soy sauce

1 tablespoon olive oil

Whisk together all the ingredients for the dressing in a small bowl.

In a large bowl, combine the cucumber, chayote and onion. Add the dressing to the vegetables and toss to coat. Add the roughly chopped parsley and mint and season with salt and pepper to taste.

CRUNCHY GREEN HOUSE SALAD

SERVES 4   PREP TIME: 10 MINUTES

Everyone needs a good 'house salad' in their arsenal. House salads aren't meant to be the heroes of the show, but most definitely shouldn't be an afterthought. This salad embraces texture from pumpkin seeds, celery, sugar snap peas and creamy avo. For salads, texture and contrast is essential. I love the mellow, refreshing crunch of a cos (romaine) lettuce and the subtle sweetness of the pear. Fruit in salads can freak people out, but they can work so wonderfully. I would serve this salad with my roasted aubergine (eggplant; see page 131)!

1 large avocado, chopped

1 head of cos (romaine) lettuce, roughly chopped

8 celery stalks, sliced diagonally

200 g (7 oz) sugar snap peas, trimmed and halved

1 cucumber, sliced into half-moons

1 Williams (Barlett) or D'Anjous pear, chopped

50 g (2 oz/⅓ cup) pumpkin seeds

FOR THE DRESSING

4 tablespoons extra virgin olive oil

juice and zest of 1 lemon

1 tablespoon Dijon mustard

1 tablespoon maple syrup

1 garlic clove, very finely chopped

handful of chives, finely chopped

salt and freshly ground black pepper

In a small bowl, whisk together all the ingredients for the dressing apart from the chives. Stir through the chives, then set aside.

Put the avocado into a large bowl with a tablespoon of the dressing and stir to coat – this will stop it turning brown. Add the rest of the ingredients along with the remaining dressing and toss well before serving.

BEETROOT HARD DOUGH BREAD PANZANELLA

SERVES 3–4   PREP TIME : 10 MINUTES   COOK TIME : 40 MINUTES

Hard dough bread will always have a special place in my heart. I have fond memories of eating it straight out of the oven from Captains Bakery in Jamaica. It's the kind of bread you can smell halfway down the street, and as you get closer to the bakery, your desire increases dramatically. For me, panzanella is the perfect use for this bread. I love how panzanella can be flexible in the vegetables used – I added roasted beetroot (beets) as the earthiness pairs well with the hard dough. This salad carries a lot of weight and can be enjoyed on its own. I'm a strict seasonal tomato eater only kinda gal, because there's nothing more disappointing than an out of season tomato. However, I feel like cherry tomatoes are safer all year round, which is why I've used them in this recipe. The tomatoes are really important to the flavour, so I would urge you to make this in tomato season when you keep the benefits of nature's divine timing.

2 large beetroot (beets), peeled and quartered

2 thick slices of hard dough bread, cut into chunks

200 g (7 oz) cherry tomatoes, halved

200 g (7 oz) radishes, sliced

handful of mint leaves, finely sliced

65 g (2¼ oz) vegan feta, crumbled

handful of basil leaves, roughly torn

olive oil, for roasting

salt and freshly ground black pepper

FOR THE DRESSING

1 garlic clove, finely chopped

3 tablespoons balsamic vinegar

2 tablespoons olive oil

juice of ½ lemon

Preheat the oven to 160°C (350°F/gas 4).

On a baking sheet, toss the beetroot with a glug of olive oil and some salt and pepper. Roast in the oven for 40 minutes.

Meanwhile, put the chunks of bread on a separate baking sheet, toss with a glug of olive oil and salt and pepper, then add to the oven to bake for 20 minutes. Remove and allow to cool slightly.

Put the tomatoes, radishes and mint into a large bowl. In a small bowl, whisk together the ingredients for the dressing and season with salt and pepper.

When the beetroot is cooked, add it to the bowl along with the toasted bread and dressing, tossing to coat everything. Now add the feta and basil leaves. Toss again, then tumble onto a large serving plate.

STICKY ORANGE ROASTED GREEN BEAN AND MANGETOUT SALAD

SERVES 4   PREP TIME : 5 MINUTES   COOK TIME : 20 MINUTES

I am a strong advocate for warm salads. Roasting more vegetables brings out their flavour but something dramatic changes when you roast green beans and mangetout (snow peas). There's something about their bitter sweetness that is amplified in the process. This salad comes together quickly, retaining some crunch in the green veggies.

Orange as the citrus in salads is criminally underrated in my opinion. Although it doesn't offer that extreme acidity that lemon does, it gives a more subtle balance between sweet and sour.

200 g (7 oz) fine green beans, topped and tailed

100 g (3½ oz) mangetout (snow peas)

60 g (2 oz/scant ½ cup) blanched hazelnuts

250 g (9 oz/1¼ cups) cooked green lentils

1 small shallot, finely sliced diced

handful of flat-leaf parsley leaves, roughly chopped, plus extra to serve

small handful of mint leaves, torn

FOR THE ORANGE DRESSING

juice and zest of 1 orange

2 tablespoons olive oil

1 tablespoon maple syrup

3 garlic cloves, very finely chopped

salt and freshly ground black pepper

Preheat the oven to 180°C (400°F/gas 6).

In a small bowl, whisk together all the ingredients for the dressing.

In a large bowl, toss the green beans and mangetout with half the dressing, then spread the vegetables out evenly on a wide baking sheet. Roast in the oven for 20 minutes, adding the hazelnuts after 10 minutes.

Once roasted, transfer the vegetables back into the bowl and add the lentils, shallot, parsley and mint. Add the remaining dressing and toss to combine. Sprinkle with a little more parsley before serving.

MY DREAM POTATO SALAD

SERVES 4–6   PREP TIME : 10 MINUTES   COOK TIME : 20 MINUTES

Potato salad can be a very sensitive topic. However, this is my book and therefore you can't judge me for what you're about to read. I call this my dream potato salad because it involves lots of spring onions (scallions), as well as raw mangetout (snow peas) and radishes for crunch. I opt for new potatoes because for me, potato salad season is a peak spring and summer dish, which happens to be new potato season. This is far from a traditional potato salad, so potato sal traditionalists, look away now! The question is, should a potato salad be mayo or oil based? The real answer is ackee curry mayo. Ackee's wonderful smooth and silky texture really lends itself to creamy dressings like this. The curry flavour is perfect as potatoes can really take a lot of flavour. This would be a great salad for a barbecue – please stand your corner on my behalf if anyone challenges you about your potato salad choices.

750 g (1 lb 10 oz) new potatoes, halved if large

200 g (7 oz) mangetout (snow peas) or sugar snap peas, sliced

200 g (7 oz) radishes, finely sliced

1 small shallot, finely sliced

1 spring onion (scallion), finely sliced

FOR THE ACKEE CURRY MAYO

200 g (7 oz) rinsed and drained ackee

1 garlic clove

1 tablespoon Jamaican curry powder

1 tablespoon olive oil

1 tablespoon white wine vinegar

salt and freshly ground black pepper

Put the potatoes into large saucepan, cover with cold water and add a good amount of salt. This is important as the potato is the star here and needs to be seasoned all the way through. Bring to the boil, then cook until just fork tender – about 15–20 minutes depending on the size of your potatoes. Once cooked, drain and then scatter across a flat baking sheet to dry out and cool to room temperature.

In a high-speed blender, blend together all the ingredients for the ackee curry mayo until completely smooth.

Combine all the vegetables in a large bowl, add the curry mayo and stir to completely coat. Cover with cling film (plastic wrap) and refrigerate until ready to serve.

GRATED BEETROOT WITH ROASTED HAZELNUTS AND OLIVE AND SCOTCH BONNET JAM

SERVES 4   PREP TIME : 15 MINUTES   COOK TIME : 10 MINUTES

If you think you don't like beetroot (beets), this salad will change your mind! Grating them offers a wonderful texture and retains that vibrant, deep purple colour. Olives are wonderful in savoury jams, as they are so abrasively salty (which is what I love about them). They hold up a fight in a jammy situation. This salad gives slaw vibes and would be perfect for a barbecue or even alongside a creamy, denser dish.

75 g (2½ oz/generous ½ cup) hazelnuts

4 beetroot (beets), coarsely grated

1 shallot, finely diced

glug of olive oil

1 tablespoon balsamic vinegar

handful of flat-leaf parsley, roughly chopped

salt and freshly ground black pepper

FOR THE OLIVE AND SCOTCH BONNET JAM

2 tablespoons olive oil

1 Scotch bonnet, very finely chopped

1 teaspoon ground allspice

4 garlic cloves, chopped

330 g (11 oz) jar of pitted black olives, drained and chopped

250 ml (8½ fl oz/1 cup) maple syrup

Preheat the oven to 160°C (350°F/gas 4). Scatter the hazelnuts on a baking sheet and roast in the oven for 10 minutes until well browned. Keep an eye on them, as they can burn quickly. Set aside.

Meanwhile, make the jam. In a frying pan (skillet), heat the olive oil over a medium heat. Add the Scotch bonnet and allspice. Fry with a pinch of salt until fragrant, then add the garlic and fry for another minute or so. Add the olives and fry for a further 2–3 minutes. Add the maple syrup and then allow to reduce until jammy, about 4–5 minutes. Set aside in a bowl.

In a large bowl, combine the grated beetroot with the shallot and toss with the olive oil, balsamic vinegar and salt and pepper to taste. Add the roasted hazelnuts and parsley and toss again.

In the base of a serving bowl, pile up the beetroot, then dress it with the jam on top and around the plate.

CRISPY RICE SALAD WITH CRUNCHY GREEN VEGETABLES AND SALTED CASHEWS

SERVES 4   PREP TIME: 10 MINUTES   COOK TIME: 6 MINUTES

This salad has a lot of character. It utilises leftover rice in the most wonderful way, creating a lively textural dynamic: spicy and crispy but with nourishing heart from the kale. I love a dish that uses leftovers – so often rice gets wasted, which is a shame. This application is a great way to whip up something new when you have a few friends over if you are lucky enough to have leftover rice.

3 tablespoons coconut oil

150 g (5 oz/1 cup) cold cooked rice

4 stalks cavolo nero (lacinato kale), torn

2 spring onions (scallions), finely chopped

350 g (12 oz) asparagus, finely sliced on the diagonal

60 g (2 oz/generous ⅓ cup) roasted and salted cashews

salt and freshly ground black pepper

FOR THE DRESSING

glug of olive oil

2 tablespoons coconut vinegar (or rice vinegar)

1 tablespoon soy sauce

1 tablespoon agave syrup

juice of 1 lime

Start by crisping up the rice. Melt the coconut oil in a frying pan (skillet) over a medium heat, then add the rice to the pan. Spread it out evenly, pressing it into the oil. Allow to cook undisturbed for 6 minutes, checking the bottom so that it doesn't burn. Remove from the heat and cover with a lid. Leave to sit for 5 minutes (this will help with removing the rice).

Whisk together the dressing ingredients in a large bowl, then add the cavolo nero. Massage with your hands to soften it a little and then add the spring onions and asparagus. Crumble the rice into the bowl and toss to coat. Taste and adjust the seasoning. Finally, add the cashews and serve.

ROMANTICISE COOKING

I was raised pulling food
out of earth. I know where
joy comes from
and how to make it.

– Yrsa Daley-Ward

FOR ONE ✻

Cooking alone.
For one.

Somehow we've been hoodwinked into believing that romantic cooking should be reserved for a lover. But it can be so liberating to dine with yourself. Set the scene: buy your favourite wine and a bouquet for the table. Light a candle. Put on a record and dance on your own.

Living through a global pandemic, I tried to hold on to the simple pleasures – the only things I could control. The world can leave you dizzy, angry, confused, exhausted. But food brings so much joy, whether you are cooking for your inner child or treating the adult you to a fancy pasta night. Food-based desires can vary so much, from a freshly baked cookie to a simple grilled cheese sandwich. I try to listen to my body in those moments.

Cooking for one is my lifeline. Spending hours on video calls, emails and in digital spaces, I always look forward to my next meal. Life is too short to wait for someone else to dine with.

WHEN IN NEED OF HARD FOOD

SERVES 1   PREP TIME : 10 MINUTES   COOK TIME : 8 MINUTES

I found myself craving hard food a lot during lockdown, missing my family and desperately missing Jamaica. These boiled dumplings are my favourite type of dumpling. Sometimes with a knob of butter and salt. Sometimes with curry. Sometimes with ackee. Sometimes with brown stew. Sometimes boiled with plantain, yam and potato. All their forms are welcome and hold a special place in my heart. For a bit more context, hard food is ground provisions (root vegetable staples) and dumplings that are typically served with stews, curries or other various delicious dishes in Jamaica.

I have worked out the perfect recipe to make dumplings for just one person. I spent a lot of time during the pandemic alone as my best friend worked away for months at a time, and missing out on that human touch and the presence of someone I love was hard to take – even if I couldn't admit it. I'm normally good at disappearing and I thrive on being alone, but for some reason that patch of time was difficult. In the warmth of spring 2021 and the thick of winter, food was the remedy. Depending on the size of my hunger I range between 2–3 dumplings per sitting, and if I felt like it, I would put some of my sourdough discard in it, which added an extra layer of flavour and depth. Add pieces of yam, plantain or sweet potato to pot with the dumplings too, if you desire them. Also, if you have one or two left over, you can fry them the next day, and they're even better!

100 g (3½ oz/generous ¾ cup) white spelt flour or plain (all-purpose) flour

a little water

salt and freshly ground black pepper

vegan block butter, to serve

Mix together the flour and a good pinch of salt, then add enough water for it just to come together. Don't add too much all at once.

Bring a small saucepan of salted water to the boil. Separate the dough into three balls, then flatten them with the palm of your hands into dumpling shapes. Add to the boiling water and cook for 6–8 minutes until cooked through. Serve with vegan butter and salt and pepper.

BEETROOT FRITTERS
WITH PEA AND AVO DIP

SERVES 1   PREP TIME : 10 MINUTES   COOK TIME : 5 MINUTES

As someone who works from home a lot, I've found solitude is best broken
up by taking the time to make myself a lovely lunch. This dish feels like a proper
treat. The spiced beetroot (beet) fritters are very light and have the most vibrant
earthy colour. Paired with the creamy, cold and bring green pea and avo dip,
it's a wonderful contrast of textures and flavour.

50 g (2 oz/½ cup) gram (chickpea) flour

1½ teaspoons baking powder

½ teaspoon smoked paprika

½ teaspoon ground coriander

½ teaspoon garlic granules

½ teaspoon ground cinnamon

½ teaspoon onion powder

1 small beetroot (beet), grated

2 spring onions (scallions), chopped

50 ml (1 ¾ fl oz/3 tablespoons) ice-cold
beer or sparkling water

2–3 tablespoons coconut oil

flaky sea salt and freshly ground
black pepper

FOR THE PEA AND AVO DIP

100 g (3½ oz/⅔ cup) frozen peas, thawed

5 mint leaves

½ avocado

juice of 1 lime

1 garlic clove

In a bowl, mix together the gram flour with the baking
powder and spices. Add the beetroot to the dry
ingredients, then mix in the ice-cold beer or sparkling
water until it is incorporated into a lovely batter.

In a frying pan (skillet), heat the coconut oil over
a medium-high heat. Quenelle the fritters using
two spoons, then fry for 3–4 minutes until crispy
on all sides. Drain on paper towels.

Meanwhile, blend all the ingredients for the dip
in a high-speed blender. Don't blend until smooth –
keep the dip slightly chunky. Spread the dip on
a plate and add the fritters on top. Sprinkle with
a little bit of flaky salt and enjoy!

TOFU LARB

SERVES 1   PREP TIME: 5 MINUTES   COOK TIME: 20 MINUTES

I crave spicy and salty things. Larb is a type of Thai salad that packs a massive punch. Traditionally, it is made with minced (ground) pork and is vibrant with lime and mint. This dish comes together so quickly, making it very lunch-friendly, and a wonderful meal to make for yourself when you want something delicious without having to break a sweat. Grating the tofu creates a similar texture to the traditional minced meat and allows it to caramelise really well in the pan. Serve this up with any leftover grain, over noodles, or with crunchy vegetables!

1 tablespoon jasmine rice

1 tablespoon coconut oil

4 white mushrooms, sliced

100 g (3½ oz) firm tofu, grated

1 small shallot, finely sliced

handful of coriander (cilantro), stalks finely chopped and leaves roughly chopped

¼ Scotch bonnet, deseeded and very finely chopped

2 garlic cloves, very finely chopped

8 mint leaves, torn

20 g (¾ oz) roasted peanuts or cashews, roughly chopped

salt

FOR THE DRESSING

1 tablespoon Green Seasoning (see page 208)

1 tablespoon vegan fish sauce

1 tablespoon brown sugar, coconut sugar or maple syrup

juice of 1 lime

TO SERVE

1 Little Gem lettuce

¼ cucumber, halved, deseeded and cut into matchsticks

1 carrot, cut into matchsticks

Heat a dry frying pan (skillet) over a medium-high heat. Add the rice and toast for 8–10 minutes until golden. Place in a mortar or spice grinder and grind to a dust.

In a small bowl, whisk together the ingredients for the dressing.

In the same frying pan, heat the coconut oil, then add the mushrooms and the grated tofu. Fry for 3–4 minutes with a good pinch of salt until caramelized. Add the shallot, coriander stalks and Scotch bonnet, and continue to fry for a further 3–4 minutes until softened. Add the garlic and fry until fragrant. Add the dressing and allow to coat the tofu and mushrooms. Remove from the heat and add the chopped coriander and torn mint leaves. Add some of the nuts.

Transfer the larb to a bowl and scatter over the remaining nuts. Arrange the vegetables around the bowl and enjoy!

MY DREAM LUNCH SANDO

SERVES 1   PREP TIME : 15 MINUTES   COOK TIME : 20 MINUTES

A good sando is one of my go-to solo lunches – this one takes a little bit more time than your standard sandwich, but it's worth the extra effort. I think yuba (dried tofu skin) is highly underused; they are sold dry and you can find them easily at your local Asian supermarket. They have this wonderful texture when pan fried and caramelised in a sticky sauce. Feel free to add some pickled onions or jalapeños to the mix here.

50 g (2 oz) yuba knots

1 tablespoon olive oil

5 stalks Tenderstem broccoli (broccolini), chopped into threes

½ small shallot, sliced into rings

handful of spinach

1 slice of vegan Cheddar cheese

splash of water

bread of your choice – I usually go for a good focaccia, ciabatta or sourdough

1 chargrilled red pepper from a jar

salt and freshly ground black pepper

vegan mayo, to serve

hot sauce of your choice, to serve

FOR THE MARINADE

1 tablespoon soy sauce

1 tablespoon barbecue sauce of your choice

2 garlic cloves, very finely chopped

Bring a saucepan of salted water to the boil and add the yuba knots. Reduce to a simmer and cook for 5 minutes until tender. Drain and dab dry with paper towels to remove any excess water.

In a small bowl, whisk together the marinade ingredients. Add the yuba and leave to marinate for 5 minutes. You can also do this the day before for a more intense flavour.

In a frying pan (skillet), heat the oil over a high heat. Once smoking, add the broccoli and shallot and fry until well charred and the broccoli is tender, about 3–4 minutes. Move to one side of the pan. Add the spinach and allow to wilt, seasoning with salt and pepper. Add the yuba knots to the other side of the pan along with the marinade and fry for 2–3 minutes until fragrant and caramelised. Season with salt and pepper to taste. Place the cheese on top of the broccoli and greens, add a splash of water to the pan, cover and leave to melt the cheese for 1–2 minutes.

Toast the bread, then add a smear of mayo and a little hot sauce. Add the chargrilled red pepper, followed by the cheesy garlic greens and then finally the fried yuba on top.

PLANTAIN AND BROWN LENTILS WITH HOT PISTACHIO AND CORN NUT DRESSING

SERVES 1   PREP TIME: 5 MINUTES   COOK TIME: 25 MINUTES

I lived off this dish in lockdown, with some ever-changing elements. It is great made with sweet potatoes, too, but I just love baking plantain until they are sticky and caramelised. I'm a texture fanatic, and sometimes when you cook for yourself, it's something you don't consider. There's something about the nutty and spicy warm dressing that feels really special – and spicy corn nuts are truly the greatest crunchy sound ever! I am obsessed with the sound they make. I always take a handful when walking by my kitchen. This recipe makes more dressing than you need, so there's plenty for other dishes – I love using it over freshly steamed rice and marinated tofu, or with noodles or avocado toast A gift that keeps on giving.

1 plantain, halved lengthways

1½ teaspoons olive oil

30 g (2 oz/2 tablespoons) pre-cooked puy lentils, preferably from a pouch

salt and freshly ground black pepper

thick, plain non-dairy yoghurt, to serve

FOR THE HOT PISTACHIO AND CORN NUT DRESSING

20 g (¾ oz/2 tablespoons) roasted pistachios

20 g (¾ oz/3 tablespoons) spicy corn nuts

60 ml (2 fl oz/¼ cup) olive oil

1 garlic clove, very finely chopped

1 teaspoon chilli flakes

2 tablespoons agave syrup

zest of 1 lemon

1 teaspoon fine salt

Preheat the oven to 180°C (400°F/gas 6) and line a baking sheet with baking parchment.

Rub the plantain halves with the olive oil and season with salt and pepper. Place the plantain flesh side down on the baking sheet and bake in the oven for 25 minutes.

Meanwhile, make the dressing. Combine the pistachios and corn nuts in a small bowl. Warm the olive oil in a saucepan over a medium heat, then add the garlic and chilli flakes and remove from the heat. Pour the warm oil mixture over the pistachios and corn nuts. Add the agave syrup, lemon zest and salt. Transfer to a clean jar.

Toss the cooked brown lentils in a little bit of the oil from the dressing. Plate up by adding a little bit of thick non-dairy yoghurt to a plate, then add the lentils and place the hot plantain on top. Drizzle over some of the dressing and finish with a pinch of salt. Enjoy!

SINGLE SERVE MAC AND CHEESE, ALL FOR ME

SERVES 1   PREP TIME : 5 MINUTES   COOK TIME : 10 MINUTES

There are very few things that are more soothing than mac and cheese. This recipe hinges on a powerful umami bomb made with sun-dried tomato oil, miso and nutritional yeast. It is super satisfying and everything happens in one pot. The pasta is cooked in milk and water, which makes the most of the starch that is released as the pasta is cooking, making a silky and luxurious sauce.

75 g (2½ oz) macaroni (or another small pasta shape like orzo)

200 ml (7 fl oz/scant 1 cup) non-dairy milk

50 ml (1 ¾ fl oz/3 tablespoons) water

pinch of salt

30 g (1 oz) vegan sharp Cheddar, grated

knob of vegan block butter (optional)

freshly ground black pepper

FOR THE UMAMI BOMB

1½ teaspoons miso paste

1½ teaspoons sun-dried tomato oil

1½ teaspoons yellow or Dijon mustard

1 tablespoon nutritional yeast

Put the pasta, milk, water and salt in a saucepan and bring to the boil, then reduce the heat to medium-low, cover and simmer for 6–7 minutes until the pasta is cooked.

In a small bowl, stir together all the ingredients for the umami bomb. Add to the pasta and stir well. Add the vegan cheese and allow to melt, then add plenty of black pepper and, if you're feeling indulgent, add a knob of vegan butter and allow to melt. Serve immediately.

CALLALOO PESTO PASTA

SERVES 1 PREP TIME : 10 MINUTES COOK TIME : 15 MINUTES

We love a dish that takes 30 minutes to cook and eat! Pesto can be such a wonderful foundation for veggies. The veg I'm using is callaloo, one of my favourite dark leafy greens. Although you can't get it fresh in the UK, even the tinned variety is packed with flavour. Incorporating it into a pesto sauce creates a more substantial and earthy flavour. Traditionally, pesto is made with Parmesan, but here I've subbed that sharp and salty flavour with white miso, which works perfectly. This is very much a weeknight-friendly dish. Please enjoy with a glass of wine, or kombucha if we're being good.

280 g (10 oz) tin of callaloo

40 g (1½ oz/¼ cup) pine nuts

1 garlic clove

60 ml (2 fl oz/¼ cup) olive oil, plus 1½ teaspoons for frying the chicken pieces

120 ml (4 fl oz/½ cup) water

1 teaspoon white miso paste

2 tablespoons nutritional yeast

1 teaspoon balsamic vinegar

30 g (1 oz) basil leaves

75 g (2½ oz) pasta shapes of your choice

90 g (3¼ oz) vegan chicken pieces

30 g (1 oz/scant ¼ cup) frozen peas

2 sun-dried tomatoes

salt and freshly ground black pepper

Drain and rinse the callaloo, then transfer to a kitchen towel, nut milk bag or muslin (cheesecloth) and squeeze to drain out any excess water.

Put the pine nuts in a cold frying pan (skillet), bring up to a medium heat and toast for 3–5 minutes until golden. Set aside.

Put the garlic, 60ml (2fl oz/¼ cup) of the olive oil and the water in a food processor and blender until smooth. Now add the miso, nutritional yeast and balsamic vinegar and blend again. Finally, add the basil and callaloo, blend once more and season with salt and pepper – I start with ½ teaspoon salt and adjust from there. Feel free to add more olive oil or water if you prefer a looser sauce.

Bring a saucepan of water to the boil and cook the pasta until al dente – 2–3 minutes less than the packet instructions.

As the pasta is boiling, heat 1½ teaspoons of olive oil in a frying pan over a medium heat and fry the vegan chicken pieces until golden brown. Season with salt and pepper.

When the pasta is just about cooked, add the peas to the pan and let them defrost for 1 minute or so. Drain the pasta, reserving some of the pasta water.

Return the pasta and peas to the pan and add some of the pesto (I use about 100 g), then loosen a little with the pasta water.

Transfer the pasta to a bowl and add the vegan chicken on top. Garnish with the sun-dried tomatoes and toasted pine nuts.

Store any leftover pesto in a clean jar in the refrigerator and use within 1–2 weeks.

ROASTED TOFU AND SQUASH WITH GREEN PEANUT SAUCED NOODLES

SERVES 1   PREP TIME : 20 MINUTES   COOK TIME : 20 MINUTES

I love making a sauce at the top end of the week that can filter into various dishes. This dressing is very rich, but when topped with roasted tofu and squash, it provides a wonderful stress-free lunch option. This makes tons of sauce, so save the leftovers to use over rice and veggies!

60 g (2 oz) soba or udon noodles

½ Little Gem lettuce, torn

2 stalks cavolo nero (lacinato kale), torn

handful of coriander (cilantro), roughly chopped

roasted and salted peanuts, for sprinkling

FOR THE TOFU

100 g (3½ oz) extra-firm tofu

1 tablespoon cornflour (cornstarch)

1 tablespoon soy sauce

½ tablespoon olive oil

1 teaspoon garlic granules

freshly ground black pepper

FOR THE SQUASH

1 wedge of butternut squash, cut into chunks

1½ teaspoons olive oil

salt and freshly ground black pepper

FOR THE GREEN PEANUT SAUCE

100 ml (3½ fl oz/scant ½ cup) coconut milk

1½ teaspoons Jamaican curry powder

1 tablespoon soy sauce

50 g (2 oz/3 tablespoons) smooth peanut butter

50 g (2 oz/1½ cups) coriander (cilantro) leaves

50 g (2 oz/1½ cups) flat-leaf parsley leaves

1 spring onion (scallion)

juice of ½ lemon

Preheat the oven to 170°C (375°F/gas 5).

First prepare the tofu. Place the tofu between two paper towels and dab it dry. Using your hands, crumble the tofu into big chunks and place in a bowl. Add the remaining ingredients and toss together to coat. Place on a baking sheet lined with baking parchment.

Put the chunks of squash on the other side of the tray. Drizzle with the olive oil and season with salt and pepper. Bake the tofu and squash in the oven for 20 minutes until the tofu is crispy and the squash is golden.

Put the ingredients for the sauce in a high-speed blender and blend until smooth. If needed, add a little water until it has reached your desired consistency. Transfer to a jar and set aside.

Cook the noodles according to the packet instructions and drain, rinsing with cold water to stop them cooking. Put the cavolo nero in a bowl and add a tablespoon of the dressing. Massage it into the kale to soften, then add the noodles and add another 2 tablespoons of the dressing. Toss together to coat. Add the Little Gem and coriander. Toss and transfer to serving bowl. Top with tofu and squash and some peanuts for crunch.

WHITE CHOCOLATE AND STEM GINGER COOKIES ... TWO FOR NOW, TWO FOR LATER

SERVES 1–2 PREP TIME : 15 MINUTES COOK TIME : 18 MINUTES

A very good cookie trumps all baked goods for me. I'm not here to argue, just laying my sweet treat desires on the table. Sometimes the concept of baking big-batch desserts alone feels like a mountain to climb. However, if you crave a cookie and you live alone, or with one other person, you deserve to have a cookie. These cookies are crisp on the outside and gooey on the inside, with savoury respite from the black pepper, miso and brown butter. They're an adult cookie that should be served with ice-cold milk and enjoyed warm straight from the oven.

1½ teaspoons chia seeds

1 tablespoon water

70 g (2¼ oz) vegan block butter

2 tablespoons caster (superfine) sugar

45 g (1¾ oz/¼ cup) light brown soft sugar

½ teaspoon vanilla extract

1½ teaspoons white miso paste

70 g (2¼ oz/generous ½ cup) plain (all-purpose) flour

½ teaspoon freshly ground black pepper

pinch of salt

¼ teaspoon bicarbonate of soda (baking soda)

80 g (3 oz) vegan white chocolate, chopped

Preheat the oven to 170°C (375°F/gas 5). Line a baking sheet with baking parchment.

Start by making the 'chia egg'. Mix together the chia seeds and the water in a small bowl and then let sit for 5 minutes.

In a saucepan, brown the butter over a medium heat for 4½ minutes until you can see little brown flecks. Transfer to a bowl and add the sugars, vanilla extract and white miso, then whisk until combined. Set aside.

In a separate bowl, combine the dry ingredients and stir to combine. Add the set chia egg to the brown butter mixture and stir. Now, using a spatula, combine the wet ingredients with the dry until it's just about incorporated. Finally, stir in the chocolate. Set aside to rest for at least 30 minutes.

Separate the dough into four balls. Set two aside, then wrap the other two in cling film (plastic wrap) and store in the freezer for later. Put the two reserved balls of dough on the prepared baking sheet and bake in the oven for 13 minutes.

SMALL-BATCH STICKY TOFFEE PUDDING

SERVES 1–2   PREP TIME : 25 MINUTES, PLUS 30 MINUTES SOAKING TIME   COOK TIME : 20 MINUTES

I spent most of lockdown thinking about sticky toffee pudding for some crazy reason. It is my favourite English dessert. Those notes of molasses and sticky date are something that I truly fantasise about. Often when you're cooking for yourself, a proper dessert feels like mission impossible – especially a steamed or baked pudding like this, where you usually have tons of leftovers. To honour my lockdown craving, I wanted to write a small-batch sticky toffee pudding recipe. One for now, one for later. Or, if you're having an intimate dinner with a friend or lover, this makes two perfect personal-sized puds.

1 tablespoon ground linseed (flaxseed)

1½ tablespoons water

2 pitted dates, chopped

60 ml (2 fl oz/¼ cup) boiling water

1 teaspoon bicarbonate of soda (baking soda)

1½ tablespoons melted coconut oil or olive oil

1 tablespoon golden (light corn) syrup

1 tablespoon black treacle (molasses)

1 tablespoon vanilla extract

1 tablespoon non-dairy milk

20 g (¾ oz/2 tablespoons) light brown soft sugar

70 g (2¼ oz/generous ½ cup) plain (all-purpose) flour

1 teaspoon baking powder

good pinch of salt

vegan block butter, for greasing

non-dairy vanilla ice cream, to serve

FOR THE CARAMEL

85 ml (3 fl oz/⅓ cup) coconut milk

85 g (3 oz/scant ½ cup) dark brown soft sugar

good pinch of salt

Preheat the oven to 170°C (375°F/gas 5). Grease two ramekins.

Start by making the 'flax egg'. Mix together the ground flaxseed and the water in a small bowl and then let sit for 5 minutes.

Put the dates into a small bowl, cover with the boiling water and set aside to soak for 30 minutes. Once softened, mash the dates a little with a spoon, then mix in the bicarbonate of soda.

In a bowl, combine the oil, golden syrup, treacle, vanilla extract, milk and sugar. In a separate bowl, mix together the flour, baking powder and salt, then combine the dry ingredients with the wet ingredients and add the dates. Mix well until fully combined.

Divide the batter between the ramekins, using your thumb to wipe around the top to create a rim. Bake in the oven for 20 minutes.

After 10 minutes, prepare the caramel. Combine the coconut milk, sugar and salt in a saucepan and bring to the boil, then continue to cook for 4–5 minutes until reduced and thickened into a caramel.

Once baked, run a knife around the puddings and tap out into a bowl. Drizzle the caramel on top and serve immediately with a scoop of ice cream.

DARK CHOCOLATE MOUSSE, ALL FOR ME

SERVES 1   PREP TIME : 5 MINUTES, PLUS 2 HOURS CHILLING TIME   COOK TIME : 1 MINUTE

I often find myself craving dark chocolate, but wanting something a bit more than just a couple of squares. Something I can sit and watch too many episodes of my latest TV obsession with … This recipe is so ridiculously simple, yet so incredibly rich and rewarding.

30 g (1 oz) vegan dark (bittersweet) chocolate

60 ml (2 fl oz/¼ cup) non-dairy double (heavy) cream

1 tablespoon tahini

1½ teaspoons agave syrup

drop of vanilla extract

RIFF-ABLE IDEAS

fold a hit of Tabasco into the mousse for a chilli-chocolate vibe

crumble sesame brittle on top

top with crushed Biscoff biscuits

add a little swig of rum/amaretto/coffee liqueur to the mixture

SEE PHOTO OVERLEAF

Break up the chocolate into a bowl and microwave on high for 1 minute, stirring every 15 seconds until melted. In a separate bowl, whip the cream to firm peaks. At this point the chocolate should have cooled enough. Add a heaped tablespoon of the whipped cream to the chocolate and mix to temper it. Add the chocolate and cream mixture to the rest of the whipped cream and fold in. Finally, add the tahini, agave syrup and vanilla extract. Fold again. Transfer to a glass, then chill in the refrigerator for at least 2 hours.

COM
FORT

GRUB

What defines 'comfort food' tends to be very broad and is usually tied to your upbringing and earliest memories. In most cases, it's the memory tied to the food that brings the comfort. When you crave your comfort dish, you have no choice but to make it. Nothing will suffice in that moment. For me, it's red pea soup and a hot patty ... curry and a flaky roti ... brown stew ... my mother's fried dumplings. Prepare to get to know me a little better through my favourite food memories.

RED PEA SOUP

Saturday soup is a ritual in most Jamaican households, and my favourite soup growing up was red pea soup. In fact, if I had to choose a last meal, this would be it. It's a hug in a bowl, and when the weather dips and the seasons switch between autumn (fall) and winter, this is the soup that I make. It is finished with a type of simple dumpling called spinners. The most important ingredient here is the time to make it. Leaving the kidney beans to soak overnight creates a buttery texture in the final soup. Be sure to chop the yam, sweet potatoes and carrots to the same size so that they cook evenly.

360 g (12½ oz/2 cups) dried kidney beans

2.5 litres (85 fl oz/10 cups) water

2 vegetable stock pots

1 tablespoon allspice berries

bunch of fresh thyme, leaves picked

3 garlic cloves, finely chopped

1 onion, diced

1 Scotch bonnet

3 spring onions (scallions), chopped

2 sweet potatoes, peeled and chopped into chunks

2 large carrots, peeled and chopped into chunks

½ large yam, peeled and chopped into chunks

400 ml (13 fl oz/generous 1½ cups) coconut milk

FOR THE SPINNERS

250 g (9 oz/2 cups) plain (all-purpose) flour

250 ml (8½ fl oz/1 cup) water

pinch of salt

Put the dried kidney beans in a bowl or saucepan, cover with water and leave to soak overnight. The beans will double in size.

The next day, start by preparing the spinners. In a bowl, mix together the flour, water and salt to form a smooth dough. Cover with cling film (plastic wrap) and set aside.

Rinse and drain the kidney beans and set aside. For the soup, combine the water and vegetable stock pots in a large saucepan and bring to the boil. Add the beans, allspice, thyme, garlic, onion and Scotch bonnet, cover and reduce to a simmer. Cook for 45–60 minutes, then add the remaining vegetables and coconut milk and allow to cook for a further 10 minutes.

Meanwhile, finish the spinners. Take a thumb-sized piece of the dough and form thin, tapered sausage shapes using the palms of your hands. Add the dumplings to the pan and cook for a further 10–15 minutes, until the dumplings are cooked.

Remove the Scotch bonnet before serving.

ONE-POT JAMMY AUBERGINE AND BULGUR

SERVES 4   PREP TIME : 10 MINUTES   COOK TIME : 1 HOUR

I live for a one pot meal, but often I find most of them that I see work better if you just make them the traditional way. This bulgur dish is a treat. The way in which you cook everything together really benefits the cooking of the aubergine. At the base of the dish there are wonderful earthy lively flavours that have enough time to come together really well. This feels very do-able on a weekday, as it's so low maintenance and just requires some chopping in the beginning.

1½ tablespoons tamarind paste

1 tablespoon soy sauce

1 tablespoon light brown soft sugar

3–4 tablespoons olive oil

1 aubergine (eggplant), cut into 8 long wedges

3 carrots, each cut into 4 long wedges

1 red onion, sliced into half-moons

4 garlic cloves, very finely chopped

2.5 cm (1 inch) piece of fresh ginger root, peeled and very finely chopped

6 allspice berries

1½ teaspoons coriander seeds, ground (or 1 teaspoon ground coriander)

400 ml (13 fl oz/generous 1½ cups) vegetable stock

160 g (5½ oz/scant 1 cup) bulgur wheat

salt and freshly ground black pepper

TO SERVE

non-dairy yoghurt

roughly chopped flat-leaf parsley

toasted hazelnuts

Preheat the oven to 180°C (400°F/gas 6).

In a small bowl, mix together the tamarind paste, soy sauce and brown sugar.

Heat the olive oil in a heavy-bottomed casserole dish (Dutch oven) with a lid over a medium heat. Fry the aubergine and carrots in batches for a few minutes on each side until they are nicely caramelised. Once fried, transfer to a bowl and set aside.

Next, add the onions to the pan and fry with a pinch of salt for 3–4 minutes until softened, then add the ginger and garlic along with the allspice and coriander seeds and fry for 3 minutes until fragrant. Add the aubergine and carrots back to the pan, then add the tamarind mixture and vegetable stock. Bring to the boil and season with salt and pepper. Cover with a lid and transfer to the oven to cook for 13–14 minutes.

After this time, remove the pan from the oven and add the bulgur, ensuring it is tucked into the liquid. Cook for a further 23 minutes, covered, until the bulgur is fluffy and cooked through. Serve family style with some yoghurt, fresh herbs and toasted hazelnuts to top.

SQUASH AND BUTTER BEAN CURRY WITH SPINNERS

SERVES 6   PREP TIME : 15 MINUTES   COOK TIME : 20 MINUTES

A good curry is the ultimate comfort grub. Imagine you come home, it's peak autumn (fall), you've been caught in the rain. What would you want to eat when you get in? For me that's a curry. With freshly steamed rice. of course! Butter (lima) beans are the bean underdog. Their creamy lush texture really holds up in this curry and contrasts beautifully with a red kuri squash, which is my personal favourite.

500 ml (17 fl oz/2 cups) vegetable stock

100 g (3½ oz) creamed coconut

4 tablespoons coconut oil

1 onion, diced

2 tablespoons medium Jamaican curry powder

1 thumb-sized piece of fresh ginger root, peeled and grated

1 bay leaf

1 tablespoon allspice berries, ground

6 garlic cloves, very finely chopped (yes, 6)

2 ½ tablespoons Green Seasoning (see page 208)

1 Scotch bonnet

100 ml (3½ fl oz/scant ½ cup) coconut milk

4 sprigs of thyme

1 x 400 g (14 oz) tin of butter (lima) beans, drained and rinsed

1 red kuri squash or other small–medium sized squash, chopped into chunks

1 potato, diced

salt and freshly ground black pepper

FOR THE SPINNERS

150 g (5 oz/1¼ cups) plain (all-purpose) flour

enough water to bring the dough together

TO SERVE

roughly chopped coriander (cilantro)

spring onions (scallions)

rice or roti

In a jug (pitcher) combine the hot stock with the creamed coconut and use a fork to break up the coconut and allow it to dissolve.

Heat the coconut oil in a deep, wide frying pan (skillet) or casserole dish (Dutch oven) over a medium heat. Add the onion with a pinch of salt and fry for 4–5 minutes until softened and caramelised. Add the curry powder, ginger, bay leaf and ground allspice. Toast for a further 2 minutes until fragrant. Next, add the garlic and green seasoning, which will add depth of flavour. Cook out for 4–5 minutes, then deglaze the pan with the stock and creamed coconut mixture. Add the whole Scotch bonnet, the coconut milk and the thyme. Bring to the boil, then add the butter beans, squash and potato. Reduce to a simmer, cover and cook for 8–10 minutes until the squash is tender.

Meanwhile, make the spinners. In a bowl, mix together the flour and water to form a smooth dough. Take a thumb-sized piece of the dough and form thin, tapered sausage shapes using the palms of your hands.

Add the dumplings to the pan and push into the curry sauce. Cover and cook for 6–8 minutes until the spinners are cooked. Check and adjust the seasoning, then serve up with fresh coriander, spring onions and rice or roti.

ACKEE CARBONARA

SERVES 3–4   PREP TIME : 15 MINUTES   COOK TIME : 10 MINUTES

Although I would never say that ackee is a replacement for eggs, it works
so well in replacing the egg yolks in a carbonara. It is so wonderfully rich just
blended on its own that it is the perfect ingredient to emulsify a sauce. Italians,
please don't come for me. But this just works on so many levels.

250 g (9 oz) rinsed and drained ackee

1 tablespoon nutritional yeast

½ teaspoon miso paste

350 g (12 oz) rigatoni

50 g (2 oz) vegan Parmesan, grated,
plus extra to serve

olive oil, for frying

salt and freshly ground black pepper

FOR THE TOFU BACON

100 g (3½ oz) smoked tofu,
cut into lardons (thin strips)

1 tablespoon liquid smoke

1 teaspoon smoked paprika

1 teaspoon garlic granules

1 teaspoon onion powder

Put the ackee, nutritional yeast and miso paste into
a pestle and mortar and pound together. Alternatively,
you can blend them if you have a small enough bowl for
your food processor. Once smooth, set aside.

Toss together all the ingredients for the tofu bacon
in a small bowl. Set aside while you cook the pasta.

Bring a large saucepan of well-salted water to the
boil and cook the rigatoni according to the packet
instructions. When it's almost al dente, add a couple
of glugs of olive oil to a large frying pan (skillet) over
a medium heat. Add the lardons and cook until crispy.

Once cooked, add the pasta to the lardons, allowing
some of the pasta water to transfer, then add the ackee
mixture. Stir over the heat to emulsify and cook for
2–3 minutes until glossy. Remove from the heat, add
the Parmesan and season with salt and pepper. Stir well.

Serve in bowls with extra Parm grated on top.

COMFORT GRUB

'OXTAIL' GRAVY WITH SPRING ONION AND ROASTED GARLIC MASH

SERVES 4   PREP TIME : 15 MINUTES   COOK TIME : 1¼ HOURS

Growing up in Jamaica, there was a small homestyle restaurant by a train line where my mum took me as a treat. I would order fried chicken with all the fixings (rice and peas, salads and plantain), and oxtail gravy on the rice. The rich oxtail gravy took the dish to the next level. This recipe honours that memory. Mash hits differently when you use baked potatoes. They retain all their deep potato flavour as they're not cooked in water, which means no excess liquid.

3 onions, quartered

3 carrots, sliced

2 tablespoons olive oil, plus extra for frying

1 tablespoon balsamic vinegar

6 king oyster mushrooms, thickly sliced

1 tablespoon tomato purée (paste)

1 tablespoon allspice berries

250 ml (8½ fl oz/1 cup) Guinness or another dark stout

1 tablespoon soy sauce

1 teaspoon Worcestershire sauce

1 tablespoon light brown soft sugar

6 garlic cloves

2 bay leaves

5 sprigs of thyme

1 x 400 g (14 oz) tin of butter (lima) beans

400 ml (13 fl oz/generous 1½ cups) vegetable stock

salt and freshly ground black pepper

FOR THE MASH

4 baking potatoes

1 bulb of garlic

50 g (2 oz) vegan block butter

50 ml (1 ¾ fl oz/3 tablespoons) non-dairy single (light) cream

3 spring onions (scallions), chopped

Preheat the oven to 160°C (350°F/gas 4).

Prick the potatoes with a fork and place on a baking sheet. Bake in the oven for 1¼ hours.

Meanwhile, put the onions and carrots into a separate baking tray (pan) with the oil and balsamic vinegar. Toss to coat, then season with salt and pepper. Add the bulb of garlic for the mash to the tray and drizzle with a little olive oil and sprinkle with salt. Bake alongside the potatoes for 20–25 minutes until the onions and carrots are caramelised and the garlic is fragrant. Remove from the oven and set aside.

In a casserole dish (Dutch oven), heat a glug of olive oil over a medium heat. Fry the mushrooms in batches for 4–5 minutes until caramelised and browned on all sides. Set aside in a bowl.

Add a little more oil to the pan, then add the roasted onions and carrots along with the tomato purée and allspice berries and fry for 2 minutes until darkened. Deglaze the pan with the stout, scraping all the good brown bits from the bottom of the pan, then add the soy sauce, Worcestershire sauce, brown sugar, garlic, bay leaves and thyme. Cook for 30 seconds or so, then add the butter beans, mushrooms and stock. Bring to the boil, then reduce the heat and simmer, covered, for 25–30 minutes, stirring occasionally, until the gravy has reduced and thickened. Taste and adjust the seasoning, adding another glug of balsamic vinegar if needed.

By now the potatoes should be ready. Squeeze out the roasted garlic and chop the cloves. In a saucepan, melt the butter and cream over a low heat. Scoop out the flesh of the potatoes and mash to combine, then add the chopped roasted garlic and spring onions and season with salt and pepper.

Serve a big dollop of mash with the oxtail gravy on top.

ODE TO BROWN STEW

Brown stew has a very special place in my heart. Its base comes from burning sugar in hot oil, which gives a deep savoury and subtly sweet note to the dish. Growing up, we normally had brown stew with chicken, but you can essentially brown stew anything. I have two brown stew dishes to share in this book, one inspired by the popular Chinese dish mapo tofu, and the other inspired by ramen – two of my favourite things to order when dining out. For me there are many crossovers with Chinese cooking and Jamaican cooking.

BROWN STEW MUSHROOMS
WITH SILKEN TOFU

SERVES 4   PREP TIME: 10 MINUTES   COOK TIME: 25 MINUTES

This dish combines my deep love for brown stew with my favourite Chinese
dish, mapo tofu. This was inspired by a mind blowing mapo tofu I had in LA at
Pine & Crane. I'm not ashamed to say that I think I went three times in a week.
Their version reminded me a lot of brown stew. I've used two different types
of mushroom in this dish. The king oyster mushrooms provide a meaty texture,
while the shiitake mushrooms give a deeper savoury flavour. This dish would
be perfect over steamed rice, which is how I grew up eating brown stew.

2 tablespoons olive oil

1 tablespoon light brown soft sugar

4 king oyster mushrooms, cut into
big chunks

300 ml (10 fl oz/1¼ cups) boiling
water or stock

200 g (7 oz) shiitake mushrooms, sliced

1 onion, diced

1 large tomato, diced

4 allspice berries

4 garlic cloves

5 sprigs of thyme

1 Scotch bonnet

1 carrot, finely sliced

300 g (10½ oz) firm silken tofu, cubed

1½ teaspoons cornflour (cornstarch)

FOR THE UMAMI PASTE

1 tablespoon tomato purée (paste)

1 tablespoon ketchup

2 teaspoons soy sauce

½ tablespoon browning

1 teaspoon balsamic vinegar

Mix together all the ingredients for the umami paste
in a small bowl and set aside.

Heat the olive oil in a deep frying pan (skillet) or casserole
dish (Dutch oven) over a medium-low heat, then add
the sugar and cook together for 30–60 seconds until
it creates a caramel. Add the oyster mushrooms and
caramelise in the mixture for 2 minutes, stirring often.
If the sugar sticks to some of the mushrooms or the
pan, that's OK, as it will be deglazed later, but add
a little of the boiling water or stock if needed.

Add the shiitake mushrooms, onion, tomato, allspice
berries, garlic, thyme and whole Scotch bonnet along
with another splash of the water/stock if required. Sauté
for 2–4 minutes until softened. Add the umami paste
and cook for a further 4–5 minutes to remove any raw
flavour from the tomato purée. Now add the remaining
boiling water/stock and deglaze the pan, using a wooden
spoon to scrape up all the brown bits from the pan. Stir
in the carrot, then add the tofu on top of the stew. Cover
and bring to the boil, then cook for 5–8 minutes until
the carrots are softened. Finally, in a small bowl, mix the
cornflour with 2 tablespoons of sauce from the pan
to make a slurry, then stir this mixture into the stew
and allow to cook out and thicken for a minute or so.

SEE PHOTO OVERLEAF

BROWN STEW NOODLE SOUP

SERVES 3   **PREP TIME : 15 MINUTES**   **COOK TIME : 2 HOURS**

I love soup, but I need lots of things in them. This is partly why I think Jamaican soup is the best – there's always a dumpling to look forward to. When I travelled to Japan in 2016, I went to a vegan ramen shop and the complex, balanced flavour of that soup was so inspiring. This is a labour of love, but it's so worth it.

FOR THE BROTH

1 sheet of kombu

100 g (3½ oz) dried shiitake or porcini mushrooms

2 carrots

2 celery stalks

1 bunch of thyme

1 tablespoon allspice berries

water, to cover

FOR THE BROWN STEW BASE

1 tablespoon vegetable oil

1 tablespoon light brown soft sugar

200 g (7 oz) shiitake mushrooms

300 g (10½ oz) chestnut (cremini) mushrooms

1 x quantity of umami paste (see page 95)

3 garlic cloves, very finely chopped

salt and freshly ground black pepper

FOR THE TOPPINGS

1 tablespoon browning

1 tablespoon soy sauce

1 tablespoon ketchup

1 tablespoon brown sugar

1 teaspoon ground allspice

300 g (10½ oz) firm tofu, cut into 3 thick slices

3 tablespoons vegetable oil, plus extra for drizzling

3 pak choi (bok choi), halved lengthways

1 corn on the cob

3 bunches of ramen noodles

finely sliced spring onions (scallions), to garnish

First make the broth. Put all the ingredients into a saucepan and cover with water. Bring to the boil and then reduce the heat and simmer for 1½ hours. Strain and transfer to a jug (pitcher).

For the brown stew base, heat the olive oil in a deep frying pan (skillet) or casserole dish (Dutch oven) over a medium-low heat, then add the sugar and cook together for 2–3 minutes until it creates a caramel. Add the mushrooms and caramelise in the mixture for 2 minutes, stirring often. If the sugar sticks to some of the mushrooms or the pan, that's OK, as it will be deglazed later, but add a little of the broth if needed. Add the umami paste and cook out for 2–3 minutes, then add the garlic and fry for 1 minute. Now deglaze with the broth, scraping up all of the brown bits, and bring to the boil. Season to taste.

Next prepare the toppings. Combine the browning, soy sauce, ketchup, sugar and allspice in a bowl, then add the sliced tofu and gently coat. Heat the vegetable oil in a frying pan over a medium heat and fry the tofu for 3–4 minutes on each side until caramelised. Remove from the pan and set aside. In the same pan, fry the halved pak choi in two batches for 3–4 minutes, seasoning with salt. Remove from the pan and set aside. Finally, add the corn and char on all sides, then remove and use a sharp knife to shave off the kernels.

Bring a saucepan of water to the boil and cook the noodles to just 1 minute shy of the packet instructions (when they are hit with the hot broth they will continue to cook a little). Drain, drizzle with a little oil and divide between bowls.

Ladle over the hot broth, then top with the tofu, pak choi and corn. Finally, sprinkle over some spring onions to garnish and serve.

RUM PUNCH

SERVES 4   PREP TIME : 10 MINUTES

This rum punch screams summer and al fresco eating. It screams barbecue season, and, most of all, it screams strawb season – and when strawb season hits, I'm eating them in abundance.

Rum punch can never be too strong, so let the spirit take you on this one. The fresh strawberry syrup adds a wonderful vibrancy and makes the whole thing dangerously addictive.

20 g (¾ oz) mint leaves

2 limes, sliced

200 ml (7 fl oz/scant 1 cup) dark or white rum

1.5 litres (50 fl oz/6½ cups) pineapple juice

lots of ice

FOR THE STRAWBERRY SYRUP

200 g (7 oz) strawberries, hulled

150 ml (5 fl oz/scant ⅔ cup) agave syrup

8 mint leaves

freshly grated nutmeg

juice of 4 limes

Start by making the fresh strawberry syrup. Blend all the ingredients together in a blender, and then strain with a sieve.

Put the mint leaves and lime slices for the punch in a big jug (pitcher). Add the strawberry syrup, rum and pineapple juice. Top up with lots of ice, stir well and serve.

DISHES FOR

SPECIAL
OCCASIONS

Dinners for big occasions often become political in families. Christmas and Easter meals are so important in my household, as everyone is normally so busy and caught up in life that it's the only time we really get to sit together as a family. However, the pressure around the food is immense.

As a teenager I took on the New Year's Day meal. I declared that I would be in charge of the food. Each year I waited patiently for the day to arrive, because it meant I could go a little off script, and do something more interesting and non-traditional. No one expects that much on New Year's Day, in comparison to the other big dinners, and I was hoping if I consistently did it well that I would transition smoothly into Christmas dinner. Which, eventually, is what happened. I remember it vividly, because I made too many things that crossed over each other, and the dinner arrived very late. It wasn't a total disaster, but it was the Christmas that everyone got hungrier and hungrier. The pressure really got to me and from that day on, I vowed to be a lot less stressed for these kinds of events. These are some foolproof big occasion dishes, which feel really special.

RICE AND PEAS ARANCINI

SERVES 6   PREP TIME : 30 MINUTES, PLUS 45 MINUTES RESTING TIME   COOK TIME : 1 HOUR

Rice and peas is a crowd pleaser, and in the right hands can be the main event, outshining the rest of its companions on a plate. But these arancini are in a league of their own. This recipe came into being by accident when I had a restaurant residency years ago. I had some leftover rice and peas, decided to turn them into arancini and the rest is history. This is my revised take on the concept, using a more traditional risotto-making technique. These would be great to make the day before and then simply fry them on the day you are serving.

400 g (14 oz) tin of kidney beans, drained and rinsed

1 litre (34 fl oz/4 cups) boiling water

2 teaspoons ground allspice

1 Scotch bonnet

2 garlic cloves, crushed

2 vegetable stock cubes

10 sprigs of thyme

350 ml (12 fl oz/1½ cups) coconut milk

1 tablespoon coconut oil

1 onion, finely diced

2 spring onions (scallions), finely chopped

300 g (10½ oz/1⅓ cups) risotto rice

100 g (3½ oz/1⅔ cups) panko breadcrumbs

100 g (3½ oz/generous ¾ cup) plain (all-purpose) flour

100 g (3½ oz) vegan Cheddar, cubed

vegetable oil, for deep-frying

salt and freshly ground black pepper

condiments or dips of your choice, to serve – I love spicy mayo

In a saucepan, combine the kidney beans, water, allspice, whole Scotch bonnet, garlic, stock cubes, thyme and 150 ml (5 fl oz/scant ⅔ cup) of the coconut milk. Bring to the boil, then reduce the heat and simmer for 10 minutes.

Melt the coconut oil in a frying pan (skillet) over a medium heat. Add the onion with a pinch of salt and pepper and sweat and soften for 3–4 minutes until fragrant. Add the rice and toast in the oil for 1 minute. Now add a ladle of the stock to the pan with the rice. Stir constantly, adding more stock when the first ladleful has evaporated. Repeat this method for 20–25 minutes until all the stock is used up and the rice is cooked. Check for seasoning and transfer the rice and peas risotto to a bowl. Cover with cling film (plastic wrap) and leave to cool for 45 minutes before shaping.

Set up a dredging station by putting the remaining coconut milk in a bowl, the panko breadcrumbs in another bowl and finally the plain flour in a another bowl. Season the flour with salt and pepper and stir to combine. Line a baking sheet with baking parchment, ready for the prepared arancini balls.

Wet your hands slightly and put a heaped tablespoon of rice and peas risotto into the palm of your hands. Put two cubes of the vegan cheese into the middle and enclose it in your palm. Roll it into a ball, then place it into the plain flour, then into the coconut milk, then into the panko breadcrumbs. Transfer the arancini to the baking sheet and repeat until all the mixture is used up.

Pour enough vegetable oil into a high-sided heavy-bottomed frying pan or saucepan to fill three-quarters of the pan and gently bring to heat. Test the temperature by using a wooden spoon – if lots of bubbles appear around it immediately, it's ready to go. Fry 2–3 arancini balls at a time for 6–8 minutes until golden and crisp. Drain on paper towels and season with a sprinkle of salt. Serve with your favourite condiments.

PATTIES

A flaky patty brings me straight back to my childhood.
As a kid I particularly loved to enjoy a freshly baked patty
with a carton of ice-cold chocolate milk. When I went vegan,
I struggled to find a vegan patty that wasn't just vegetable
based, so naturally a vegan chicken patty and a beef patty
were the first two things I recipe tested.

I chose to put these two patty recipes in the special occasions
chapter because these patties are a labour of love. But I promise
that they are worth it. Take the time and do this in batches,
maybe even with a friend or lover. Make a moment out of the
recipe and enjoy the process. Maybe even with a glass
of ice-cold chocolate milk.

CURRY 'CHICKEN' PATTIES

MAKES 6 PATTIES   PREP TIME : 40 MINUTES, PLUS 2½ HOURS CHILLING AND RESTING TIME   COOK TIME : 55 MINUTES

360 g (12½ oz) vegan chicken pieces

2½ tablespoons Jamaican curry powder

4 tablespoons olive oil

1 onion, diced

1 teaspoon ground allspice

2 carrots, chopped

1 spring onion (scallion), chopped

3 garlic cloves, very finely chopped

480 ml (17 fl oz/scant 2 cups) boiling water

½ teaspoon coconut sugar

1½ teaspoons black treacle (molasses)

200 ml (7 fl oz/scant 1 cup) coconut milk, plus extra for brushing

1 Scotch bonnet

a few sprigs of thyme, leaves roughly chopped

1 potato, cubed

FOR THE PATTY PASTRY

215 g (7½ oz) vegan block butter

400 g (3¼ cups) plain (all-purpose) flour

4 teaspoons ground turmeric

¾ teaspoon salt

1½ teaspoons caster (superfine) sugar

200 ml (7 fl oz/scant 1 cup) cold water

DAY 1

First, make the pastry. Cut the butter into two pieces of 95 g (3½ oz) and 120 g (4 oz) and freeze the 50 g block for 15–20 minutes, then cube it and keep it cold in the refrigerator.

In a food processor, combine the flour, turmeric, salt and sugar. Blitz until combined. Add the cold, cubed butter and blitz until the mixture resembles breadcrumbs. Slowly stream in the water and blend until it comes together as a dough. Wrap in cling film (plastic wrap) and rest for 1 hour in the refrigerator.

Meanwhile, make the filling. Toss the vegan chicken with 2 tablespoons of the curry powder and 1 tablespoon of the olive oil. Fry the pieces in a frying pan over a medium heat for 2–3 minutes until golden on each side – you may need to do this in batches. Set aside in a bowl.

Add the remaining olive oil and the onion to the pan and fry for 2–3 minutes until softened, then add the remaining curry powder and the allspice and fry for 1 minute more. Add the carrots and spring onion and fry for 2 minutes. Add the garlic and fry for a further 1 minute until fragrant.

In a measuring jug, mix together the boiling water with the coconut sugar and treacle. Deglaze the pan with it, stirring to scrape up all the brown bits. Add the coconut milk, whole scotch bonnet and thyme. Bring to the boil, then add the vegan chicken and potato and simmer, covered, for 10–15 minutes until the potato is tender. Remove from the heat, transfer to a bowl and allow to cool for 15 minutes, then transfer to the refrigerator to cool completely.

DAY 2

Freeze the remaining butter in two blocks of 60 g (2 oz) for 15–20 minutes.

Remove the pastry from the refrigerator and roll it into a rectangle, then grate one of the blocks of butter over the top to cover. Fold over either side of the pastry rectangle to meet in the middle, sealing in the edges. Then, fold again in the other direction. Seal together, wrap in cling film and rest in the refrigerator for at least 30 minutes. Repeat the process with the other block of butter.

Preheat the oven to 180°C (400°F/gas 6).

Roll out the pastry on a lightly floured surface to about 5 mm (¼ inch) thick. Cut out as many circles as you can for the patties. Add a heaped tablespoon of the curry chicken mixture onto one half of each circle leaving a 1.5 cm (½ inch) gap around the edge. Brush with a little bit of coconut milk, fold the empty half of the pastry over the filled side and crimp. Repeat until you've made all the patties. Place the patties on a baking tray and brush with coconut milk. Bake for 15–20 minutes until golden and flaky.

CHEESY 'BEEF' PATTIES

MAKES 6 PATTIES   PREP TIME : 10 MINUTES, PLUS COOLING TIME   COOK TIME : 60 MINUTES

2 tablespoons olive oil or coconut oil

1 onion, diced

3 spring onions (scallions), finely sliced

2 teaspoons ground allspice

3 garlic cloves, finely chopped

1 Scotch bonnet, deseeded
and finely chopped

200 g (7 oz) vegan minced (ground) beef

150 ml (5 fl oz/scant ⅔ cup) boiling water

2 sprigs of thyme, leaves chopped

1 x recipe quantity Patty Pastry
(see page 108)

3 slices of vegan Cheddar, halved

non-dairy milk, for brushing

salt and freshly ground black pepper

FOR THE FLAVOUR PASTE

1 tablespoon soy sauce

1 tablespoon tomato purée (paste)

1 tablespoon molasses

1 tablespoon white miso paste

First make the flavour paste by whisking together all the ingredients in a small bowl.

Heat the olive oil or coconut oil in a frying pan (skillet) over a medium heat and sweat the onions for 5 minutes with a good pinch of salt. Next add the allspice, garlic and Scotch bonnet and allow to soften for 2 minutes. Add the flavour paste and cook out for another 2 minutes. Add the vegan minced beef, then deglaze the pan with the boiling water. Bring to the boil, then reduce the heat to a simmer, add the sprigs of thyme and allow to cook, covered, for 15–20 minutes until reduced. You want the mixture to be thick and saucy, so reduce further or top up with more water as needed. Season with salt and pepper to taste, then transfer to a bowl and allow to cool.

Preheat the oven to 180°C (400°F/gas 6).

Roll out the pastry on a lightly floured surface to about 5 mm (¼ inch) thick. Cut out as many circles as you can for the patties. Add a heaped tablespoon of the beef mixture onto one half of each circle leaving a 1.5 cm (½inch) gap around the edge, then top with the cheese. Brush with a little bit of water, fold the empty half of the pastry over the filled side and crimp. Repeat until you've made all the patties. Place the patties on a baking tray and brush with a little non-dairy milk. Bake for 15–20 minutes until golden and flaky.

CALLALOO AND PLANTAIN FILO PIE

SERVES 8   PREP TIME : 15 MINUTES   COOK TIME : 55 MINUTES

I love a filo pie. My friend makes the best *bastilla*, which is an amazing
North African savoury pie and this is loosely inspired by her. Callaloo works
so well in pastry, being a heartier green, it holds its shape and doesn't wilt that
much. This would be a perfect Easter dish to bring to the family table. I know
the weight of bringing the 'vegan' dish, but this one is very flavoursome and
the plantain acts as a lovely sweet surprise. Everyone will be asking you
to make it the following year.

2 ripe plantains, sliced

2 shallots, chopped

6 garlic cloves, very finely chopped

500 g (1 lb 2 oz) drained
and rinsed tinned callaloo

juice of 1 lemon

1 tablespoon nutritional yeast

300 g (10½ oz) silken tofu

50 g (2 oz) vegan block butter

1 x 270 g (10 oz) packet of filo pastry

100 g (3½ oz) vegan Cheddar, grated

olive oil, for frying

salt and freshly ground black pepper

Preheat the oven to 170°C (375°F/gas 5).

Heat a glug of olive oil in a frying pan (skillet) over
a medium heat and fry the plantains for 3–4 minutes
until golden brown on both sides. Drain on paper
towels and season with salt.

In the same pan, fry the diced shallots with a good
pinch of salt for 3–4 minutes until softened. Add the
garlic and fry until fragrant, then add the callaloo and
toss to combine. Season, then add the lemon juice
and nutritional yeast. Add the tofu and toss together
until combined. Remove from the heat and set aside
to cool.

Brush a pie dish with some of the butter, then layer filo
pastry in the bottom of the dish, brushing with butter
between each later and rotating the sheets as you go.

Fill with half of the plantain and then add half of the
callaloo mixture on top. Sprinkle with half of the cheese.
Repeat with the remaining fillings, then fold the excess
pastry over the top to seal. Brush more butter, then
sprinkle with salt and pepper.

Bake in the oven for 45 minutes until golden and crisp.

✳✳✳✳✳

KING OYSTER MUSHROOM 'SCALLOPS' WITH COCONUT RUNDOWN RISOTTO

SERVES 2 PREP TIME : 10 MINUTES, PLUS 20 MINUTES MARINATING TIME COOK TIME : 40 MINUTES

This is very much a date-night dish. Risotto feels romantic to me, though I first had it in a bougie French restaurant when I was being schmoozed by a record label. It was a scallop risotto, and 19-year-old me hated it and got a McDonald's afterwards. Adult Denai is different. Schmooze your lover and make this for them!

DISHES FOR SPECIAL OCCASIONS

2 king oyster mushrooms

30 g (1 oz) creamed coconut

500 ml (17 fl oz/2 cups) hot vegetable stock

2 tablespoons olive oil

½ red (bell) pepper, diced

1 small onion, diced

1 teaspoon ground allspice

½ Scotch bonnet, deseeded and finely chopped

2 teaspoons chopped thyme leaves

4 garlic cloves, very finely chopped

150 g (5 oz/generous ⅔ cup) risotto rice

80 ml (3 fl oz/⅓ cup) white wine

juice of ½ lemon

handful of flat-leaf parsley leaves, roughly chopped

1 tablespoon vegan block butter

1 tablespoon nori flakes

salt and freshly ground black pepper

FOR THE MARINADE

120 ml (4 fl oz/½ cup) boiling water mixed with 1 tablespoon white miso paste

2 tablespoons apple cider vinegar

2 tablespoon nori flakes

1 tablespoon soy sauce

First, mix together all the ingredients for the marinade in a bowl. Prepare the 'scallops' by cutting the top and bottom off each king oyster mushroom, then cutting 3–4 scallops from each stem, trimming if needed. Use a sharp knife to score a hatched pattern on each scallop, being careful not to cut all the way through. Place the scallops in the marinade and mix well to coat, then leave to marinate for at least 20 minutes.

In a saucepan, dissolve the creamed coconut in the hot stock and then set aside. I've found using a fork helps to dissolve the creamed coconut.

In a deep frying pan (skillet), heat 1 tablespoon of the olive oil over a medium heat and sauté the red pepper and onion with a pinch of salt for 3–4 minutes until softened. Add the allspice, Scotch bonnet, thyme and garlic. Fry for a couple of minutes until fragrant, then add the rice and allow it to toast for a minute. Deglaze the pan with the white wine, stirring as it evaporates.

Turn down the heat to low-medium and add a ladle of hot stock and a good pinch of salt to the pan. Let the rice simmer gently, adding the stock a ladleful at a time and stirring after each addition to allow each ladleful to be absorbed before adding the next. Repeat until there's no more stock left. This process should take 15–20 minutes. When the rice is tender but still has a bit of bite, remove the pan from the heat, season with salt and pepper and finish with the lemon juice and parsley.

In a separate pan, heat the remaining tablespoon of olive oil with the vegan butter over a medium heat. Fry the mushroom scallops for 3–4 minutes on each side until caramelised, seasoning with a touch of salt and pepper, squeeze of lemon juice, then the tablespoon of nori.

Divide the risotto between two bowls, then top with the scallops.

PLANTAIN GNOCCHI WITH ROASTED GARLIC AND COCONUT MILK

SERVES 3   PREP TIME : 30 MINUTES   COOK TIME : 40 MINUTES

Making pasta and gnocchi from scratch is actually not as difficult as you
might think. Normally made with mashed potatoes, this plantain gnocchi feels
so luxurious, and indeed special. I absolutely love roasted garlic, so whenever
the oven is on I roast a bulb so that I have easy access to it in the coming days.
This sauce is mainly a combination of roasted garlic and coconut milk,
so it is very rich.

FOR THE GNOCCHI

2 ripe plantains

3 tablespoons olive oil, plus extra for
roasting the garlic and frying the gnocchi

1 teaspoon salt

100 g (3½ oz/generous ¾ cup) plain
(all-purpose) flour, plus extra for dusting

grated vegan Parmesan, to serve

FOR THE SAUCE

1 bulb of garlic

400 ml (13 fl oz/generous 1½ cups)
coconut milk

1 tablespoon nutritional yeast

1 tablespoon white miso paste

1 tablespoon coconut vinegar
or lemon juice

1 teaspoon ground allspice

olive oil, for frying

salt and freshly ground black pepper

Preheat the oven to 180°C (400°F/gas 6).

Put the plantains on a baking sheet and pierce them with
a knife to allow steam to escape. Put the bulb of garlic for
the sauce next to them and rub with a little olive oil and
some salt. Roast in the oven for 30 minutes.

Once cooked, remove the flesh from the plantains,
transfer it to a bowl and leave to cool. Once cooled,
blend in a food processor with the olive oil and salt until
smooth. Now add the flour and blend until it forms a dough.
Transfer to a lightly floured work surface and separate the
dough into two. Roll each piece into a log, then cut 2.5 cm
(1 inch) gnocchi from the logs. Press with a fork to get that
classic shape.

Squeeze the roasted garlic into a high-speed blender
and add the remaining ingredients for the sauce.
Blend until smooth.

Heat a glug of olive oil in a frying pan (skillet) over
a medium high heat. Fry the gnocchi on both sides
for 4-5 minutes until lovely and caramelised.

Pour the sauce into the frying pan with the gnocchi
and reduce over a high heat for 3–4 minutes, so that the
sauce clings to the gnocchi. Divide between bowls and
top with more black pepper and grated vegan Parmesan.

MY IDEAL BIRTHDAY CAKE

SERVES 15   PREP TIME : 25 MINUTES, PLUS 1 HOUR SOAKING   COOK TIME : 35 MINUTES

Birthdays are bittersweet for me. As an introvert I get so anxious about the
pressure to do something big and have lots of people around. However, I never
fail to have cake on my birthday. All through my twenties, regardless of what
I ended up planning, I would order myself cake or some cupcakes from my
favourite vegan bakery. I wanted to make my ideal birthday cake recipe, not
just so my friends would take the hint and make me this exact cake, but also for
the girls like me who suck at decorating cakes. This sour cherry and hazelnut
cake with dark chocolate cream cheese icing (frosting) is very forgiving as it all
happens in one tray, but still feels very adult and sophisticated.

150 g (5 oz/1 cup) dried sour cherries

amaretto, for soaking the cherries

200 g (7 oz/scant 2 cups) plain
(all-purpose) flour

200 g (7 oz/2 cups) ground hazelnuts

200 g (7 oz/scant 1 cup) cane sugar

zest of 1 lemon

1½ teaspoons baking powder

¼ teaspoon salt

200 g (7 oz) room temperature vegan
block butter, cubed

125 ml (4 fl oz/½ cup) soya milk

50 g (2 oz) silken tofu

1 tablespoon vanilla extract

1½ tablespoons plain non-dairy yoghurt

toasted hazelnuts, to decorate

FOR THE DARK CHOCOLATE CREAM CHEESE ICING

150 g (5 oz) 70% vegan dark
(bittersweet) chocolate, plus extra for
decoration

250 g (9 oz) room-temperature vegan
cream cheese

200 g (7 oz/generous 1½ cups) icing
(confectioners') sugar, sifted

1½ teaspoons vanilla extract

Put the cherries into a bowl and cover with enough
amaretto to just cover them. Leave to soak and plump
up overnight, or for at least 1 hour.

Preheat the oven to 160°C (350°F/gas 4). Grease
a 32 cm (12½ inch) baking tray (pan) and line the
base with baking parchment.

Sift the flour into the bowl of a stand mixer and add
the hazelnut flour, sugar, lemon zest, baking powder
and salt, then gently whisk attachment until combined.
On a low speed, add the cubed butter to the dry ingredients
and whisk until it resembles breadcrumbs. Try to not
overwork it.

In a food processor or using a whisk, blend together the
milk, tofu, vanilla extract and yoghurt until smooth. Add
the milk mixture gradually to the flour and butter mixture
and whisk until it comes together into a batter.

Drain the amaretto, reserving 2 tablespoons, from the
cherries. Use a spatula to fold in the soaked cherries and
reserved amaretto into the batter. Pour the batter into
the prepared baking tray and spread it out evenly with
a spatula. Lightly tap the tray on your work surface
to get rid of any air bubbles.

Place the cake in the middle of the oven and bake for
30–35 minutes, until a cocktail stick (toothpick) inserted
into the centre comes out clean.

Remove from the oven and allow to cool completely
before icing. I recommend letting it come to room
temperature and then refrigerating for at least 2 hours.

Meanwhile, make the icing. Break the dark chocolate into
a heatproof bowl over a saucepan of gently simmering
water and melt the chocolate until silky smooth. Remove
the bowl from the heat and leave to cool for 10 minutes.

In a stand mixer or using a hand-held whisk, whisk the cream cheese, then slowly add the icing sugar a tablespoon at a time until fully combined. Finally, fold in the chocolate and vanilla extract.

Cover the cooled sponge with the icing and decorate with chocolate shavings and hazelnuts. Set aside in the refrigerator, then when you're ready to serve, ensure that it comes to room temperature.

PEANUT PUNCH

SERVES 6   PREP TIME: 5 MINUTES   COOK TIME: 15 MINUTES

This peanut punch is a slightly more adult version of the traditional Jamaican drink. Roasting the peanuts adds an extra depth. There's something that's quite Christmassy about this drink, which is exactly why it's in the special occasion chapter. Enjoy on its own, with lots of ice, a swig of rum and a slice of rum cake.

160 g (5½ oz/1 cup) blanched peanuts

375–500 ml (13–17 fl oz/1½–2 cups) filtered water

250 ml (8½ fl oz/1 cup) coconut milk

5 tablespoons coconut sugar or brown sugar

1 tablespoon nutritional yeast

½ teaspoon black treacle (molasses)

1 teaspoon vanilla extract

pinch of salt

freshly grated nutmeg, to taste, plus extra to serve

TO SERVE

plenty of ice

dark rum (optional)

Preheat the oven to 180°C (400°F/gas 6). Spread out the peanuts on a baking sheet – make sure they are in one layer, so if needed use two separate sheets. Toast in the oven for 13–15 minutes until deeply golden, checking after 10 minutes and shaking the tray to turn over the peanuts. Remove from the oven and leave to cool for 15 minutes.

Transfer the nuts to a high-speed blender along with the remaining ingredients and blend until totally smooth – it should be a milkshake consistency. Strain using a nut milk bag or muslin (cheesecloth).

Serve the peanut punch with lots of ice and a sprinkle of nutmeg on top – you can even add a shot of dark rum if you're being extra indulgent.

Store in a jug (pitcher) or jar in the refrigerator for up to 1 week.

DISHES FOR SPECIAL OCCASIONS

FOOD

FOR COMPANY

The pressure of being a host can feel overwhelming. However, I shamelessly thrive on compliments about my food. I like to think of myself as quite self-assured, but there is no better compliment than someone you love enjoying your cooking in your presence. Also, it's OK to not be on schedule (I'm reminding myself here). Dinner at 7 p.m. that actually starts at 8:30 p.m.? It really doesn't matter! Let the night evolve and go with the flow. (Again, I'm talking to myself.)

When entertaining, I tend to veer towards small plates, a couple of sides, something green and bright and then the main event, so that everyone can make their own plates. This chapter is my suggestion for dishes to add to your hostation (hosting rotation). Please cook them for your very best company, add your favourite bottle of wine into the mix – maybe even a board game to throw some mild chaos into the evening – and serve some grapes and olives and a pre-dinner snack (very good combo, please try!). And remember, never skip dessert!

SORREL HOISIN FRIED 'CHICKEN' BURGER

SERVES 6   PREP TIME: 20 MINUTES, PLUS 20 MINUTES MARINATING TIME   COOK TIME: 30 MINUTES

Every now and then you need a good burger in your life, and this one satisfies that craving. This is the kind of dish I make for my non-vegan friends. The sorrel hoisin glaze is quietly delicious and adds a fruity twist. Lettuce and pickles are non-negotiable here. There's just something about the hot, crispy, sticky glazed oyster mushrooms and the ice-cold lettuce.

250 g (9 oz) oyster mushrooms

2 tablespoons Green Seasoning (see page 208)

1 tablespoon soy sauce

1 tablespoon ground allspice

vegetable oil, for deep-frying

1 x quantity Sorrel Hoisin Glaze (see page 209)

salt and freshly ground black pepper

FOR THE WET DREDGE

400 ml (13 fl oz/generous 1½ cups) soya milk

1 tablespoon lemon juice

2 tablespoons hot sauce of your choice

FOR THE CRISPY COATING

200 g (7 oz/1⅔ cups) plain (all-purpose) flour

50 g (2 oz/scant ½ cup) cornflour (cornstarch)

1 tablespoon all-purpose seasoning

1 teaspoon dried sage

1 teaspoon ground allspice

1½ teaspoons onion powder

1½ teaspoons garlic granules

TO SERVE

6 vegan-friendly brioche burger buns

knob of vegan block butter

vegan mayonnaise

½ iceberg lettuce

gherkins (pickles)

In a bowl, toss the mushrooms with the green seasoning, soy sauce, allspice and some salt and pepper. Set aside to marinate for 20 minutes.

Combine the wet dredge ingredients in one bowl and the crispy coating ingredients in another, seasoning the coating mix with plenty of salt and pepper.

Add a little of the wet dredge to the dry coating and mix in – this will create small lumps, which will become crispy pockets. Dip the mushrooms in the wet dredge, then into the coating mix and then repeat for a double coating. Tap off any excess coating mix and set aside on a baking sheet, ready to fry.

Pour enough vegetable oil into a high-sided heavy-bottomed frying pan (skillet) or saucepan to fill to halfway and gently bring to heat. Test the temperature by using a wooden spoon – if lots of bubbles appear around it immediately, it's ready to go.

Add 4–5 mushrooms to the pan, taking care not to overcrowd. Fry for 5–6 minutes until crisp and golden. Drain off any excess oil on a wire rack. Repeat until all the mushrooms are cooked. Brush the sorrel hoisin glaze on the mushrooms and set aside.

Toast the brioche buns with a touch of vegan butter.

On the base of each bun spread a tablespoon of vegan mayonnaise and add a couple of lettuce leaves. Now add the glazed mushrooms and pickles. And another dollop of vegan mayo on the top bun. Serve and enjoy!

SQUASH CUTLETS WITH VIBRANT GREEN CURRY

SERVES 4   PREP TIME: 20 MINUTES   COOK TIME: 25 MINUTES

This vibrant green curry sauce is herby and punchy from all the fresh aromatics.
It goes brilliantly with panko-coated squash, which is one of my favourite ways
to prepare squash. Preheating the baking tray (pan) with the oil provides
maximum crispiness without having to use so much oil. Serve this with some
cold thinly sliced cucumber or Pickled Cho Cho (see page 211) and
freshly steamed rice.

4 tablespoons coconut oil

200 ml (7 fl oz/scant 1 cup) soya milk

1 tablespoon lemon juice

200 g (7 oz/1⅔ cups) plain
(all-purpose) flour

1 tablespoon all-purpose seasoning

200 g (7 oz/3⅓ cups) panko breadcrumbs

1 red kuri squash, cut into thick slices

salt and freshly ground black pepper

sliced red chilli, to serve

FOR THE VIBRANT GREEN CURRY SAUCE

400 ml (13 fl oz/generous 1½ cups)
coconut milk

25 g (¾ oz/½ cup) roughly chopped
coriander (cilantro) leaves

15 g (½ oz/¼ cup) roughly chopped chives

2 garlic cloves

1 thumb-sized piece of fresh ginger root

1 teaspoon salt

3 tablespoons lemon juice

1 tablespoon Jamaican curry powder

1½ teaspoons agave or maple syrup

Preheat the oven to 170°C (375°F/gas 5).

Put the coconut oil in a baking tray (pan) and place
in the oven to preheat.

In a bowl, combine the soya milk with the lemon juice and
season with salt and pepper. In a separate bowl, combine
the flour and all-purpose seasoning, then put the panko
breadcrumbs in another bowl.

Dip the squash slices in the milk mixture, then into the
flour, then back into the milk and finally in the panko.
Set aside on a wire rack and repeat until all the squash
is coated.

Remove the hot tray from the oven and add the squash.
Return to the oven and bake for 15 minutes, then flip over
and bake for a further 10 minutes.

Meanwhile, blend all the ingredients for the curry sauce
in a food processor until completely smooth, then transfer
to a frying pan (skillet). Bring to the boil, then simmer for
5–6 minutes until reduced and intensified.

Serve the crispy coated squash with the curry sauce,
scattered with sliced chillies.

IT'S A PIZZA PARTY

SERVES 6 PREP TIME : 30 MINUTES, PLUS 2½ HOURS PROVING TIME COOK TIME : 1 HOUR

Not only did I reignite my sourdough journey in lockdown, I also bought a pizza oven. So I completed lockdown with flying colours. Pizza seems to be the ultimate gathering food. It's universally liked and is a safe option to please multiple guests (despite the whole pineapple discourse ... I promise you, liking or not liking pineapple on pizza doesn't need to be attached to your personality or in your Hinge bio). This is coming from a pineapple on pizza advocate. Most people rarely seem to make pizza at home even though its actually quite easy. The dough uses minimal ingredients and the toppings can be totally customisable to your desired flavour combinations. This is a deep-dish style pizza, which for me gets the best results when baking in a home oven.

FOR THE DOUGH

250 ml (8½ fl oz/1 cup) room-temperature water

100 ml (3½ fl oz/scant ½ cup) boiling water

1½ teaspoons maple syrup

2 teaspoons active dry yeast

400 g (14 oz/3¼ cups) strong white bread flour

1 teaspoon salt

65 ml (2½ fl oz/scant ½ cup) olive oil, plus extra for greasing

FOR THE CARAMELISED ONIONS

2 onions, sliced into half-moons

1 teaspoon fennel seeds

1 teaspoon chilli flakes, plus extra to serve

FOR THE TOFU GARLIC CREAM

150 g (5 oz) silken tofu

2 garlic cloves

salt and freshly ground black pepper

FOR THE CALLALOO TOPPING

150 g (5 oz) drained and rinsed tinned callaloo

1 tablespoon nutritional yeast

1 tablespoon balsamic vinegar

20 g (¾ oz) vegan Parmesan

1 ball vegan mozzarella, sliced

Mix the room-temperature water with the boiling water in a jug (pitcher). This will create the perfect temperature for the yeast. Add the maple syrup and yeast, mix to combine and then leave to activate for 4–5 minutes until foamy. Meanwhile, combine the flour and salt in the bowl of a stand mixer.

Add the yeast mixture to the flour along with 1 tablespoon of the olive oil and then knead with the dough hook on a medium speed for 5–6 minutes until elastic and smooth. You can also do this with your hands, kneading for 8–10 minutes. Lightly oil a bowl and transfer the dough to it. Cover with cling film (plastic wrap) and leave to rise at room temperature for 1½ hours, or until doubled in size.

As the dough is rising, get the toppings ready. Heat a generous glug of olive oil in a frying pan (skillet) over a medium heat and fry the onions, fennel seeds and chilli flakes with a big pinch of salt. Cook for 30 minutes until caramelised, then set aside.

Blend together the ingredients for the tofu garlic cream in a food processor until smooth and mix together the ingredients for the callaloo topping, apart from the vegan mozzarella, in a bowl.

Once the dough has risen, knock the air out of it. Pour the remaining olive oil into to a deep 23 cm (9 inch) rectangular baking tray (pan). Add the dough and stretch it to fit. Cover again with cling film and leave for a further 1 hour until doubled in size again. As it is rising, preheat the oven to as hot as it will go for at least 45 minutes.

Once ready, top the pizza. Start by adding three-quarters of the caramelised onions, then top with some of the tofu garlic cream. Add the callaloo and then the vegan mozzarella. Sprinkle with chilli flakes and a drizzle of olive oil and bake for 25 minutes until lovely and caramelised. Add the rest of the caramelised onions just before serving.

LOADED PLANTAIN
BOAT SPREAD

SERVES 4   PREP TIME: 5 MINUTES   COOK TIME: 35 MINUTES

I love a good spread. This plantain boat recipe gives everyone their own
individual roasted plantain to load up, adding the combinations of flavours that
they want. It's stress-free as it all comes together on a single baking sheet, giving
you time to enjoy a relaxed hosting experience.

3 tablespoons soy sauce

1 tablespoon balsamic vinegar

3 tablespoons olive oil

1 teaspoon thyme leaves

1 teaspoon smoked paprika

1 garlic clove, very finely chopped
or 1 teaspoon of garlic granules

400 g (14 oz) oyster mushrooms,
torn into shreds

1 onion, sliced into half-moons

4 plantains

salt and freshly ground black pepper

TO SERVE

grated vegan cheese

non-dairy sour cream

smashed avocado

hummus

Preheat the oven to 180°C (400°F/gas 6) and line a baking
sheet with baking parchment.

In a bowl, mix together the soy sauce, balsamic vinegar,
2 tablespoons of the olive oil, the thyme leaves, smoked
paprika, garlic and salt and pepper. Put the oyster
mushrooms and onion on one half of the baking sheet
and pour over the marinade. Mix to coat, then set aside.

Pierce the plantains with a knife or fork and place on the
sheet alongside the mushrooms. Bake in the oven for
25 minutes, then slice the plantains through the skin
down the middle, exposing the flesh. Brush with the
remaining olive oil and cook for a further 10 minutes.
Stuff the plantains with the mushrooms and onions
and serve with the toppings of your choice.

BUTTERFLY AUBERGINE WITH SPRING ONION SALSA

SERVES 4   PREP TIME : 10 MINUTES, PLUS 30 MINUTES MARINATING TIME   COOK TIME : 45 MINUTES

When aubergine (eggplant) is cooked to perfection, it can be a wonderful thing.
However, when it's undercooked, there's truly nothing worse. Generally speaking,
I think aubergine cooks the best in the oven. It's a very forgiving process this way
and gives you that lush creamy aubergine texture you dream of!

2 aubergines (eggplants)

2 tablespoons soy sauce

2 tablespoons olive oil

2 garlic cloves, very finely chopped

2 teaspoons ground allspice

2 teaspoons ground coriander

good pinch of salt

10 grinds of black pepper

1 tablespoon maple syrup

FOR THE SPRING ONION SALSA

10 spring onions (scallions),
sliced in half lengthways

2 tablespoons olive oil

3 tablespoons balsamic vinegar

pinch of cayenne pepper

handful of flat-leaf parsley leaves, chopped

salt and freshly ground black pepper

Preheat the oven to 180°C (400°F/gas 6).

Prepare the aubergines by slicing it into 4–6 even slices
down the middle, leaving the stalk intact, to create a fan
shape. Mix together the remaining ingredients except
for the maple syrup to make a marinade, then massage
it into the aubergines. Leave to marinate for 30 minutes.

For the spring onion salsa, heat 1 tablespoon of the olive
oil in a frying pan (skillet) over a high heat and add the
spring onions. Place a plate on top that fits in the pan
to press it down. Fry for 2–3 minutes, flipping once, until
caramelised on each side. Remove from the pan and
chop very finely, then transfer to a bowl with all the other
ingredients and season to taste with salt and pepper.

On a baking tray (pan) fan out the aubergines (reserving
any marinade in the bowl) and then cover with foil. Bake
in the oven for 25 minutes, then remove the foil and flip
over the aubergine. Stir the maple syrup into the leftover
marinade and use it to baste the aubergines, then bake
for a further 15 minutes until soft and caramelised. Serve
on a big plate and pour over the spring onion salsa!

SEE PHOTO ON PAGE 135

CRISPY OYSTER MUSHROOMS WITH SCOTCH BONNET BURNT LIME DRESSING AND COCONUT RICE

SERVES 4   PREP TIME : 30 MINUTES, PLUS 40 MINUTES RESTING TIME   COOK TIME : 40 MINUTES

Fried chicken and rice is very nostalgic for me. My mother's was famous in our house and she would always serve it with a slaw on the side. This recipe replaces the chicken with crispy oyster mushrooms that are similar to those I use in my fried 'chicken' burger (see page 124). Oyster mushrooms have such a succulent and juicy texture, that when fried they are reminiscent of chicken. They are really in their green jackfruit circa 2016 era, and it is truly deserved. Mushrooms in general are so magical, and I could totally imagine this working really well with a vast variety of them. The burnt lime in the dressing is so deeply savoury and offers a slight bitterness.

FOR THE COCONUT RICE

300 g (10½ oz/1½ cups) Thai fragrant (jasmine) rice or basmati rice

550 ml (18½ fl oz/2¼ cups) water

100 g (3½oz) creamed coconut (or desiccated/dried shredded coconut)

1½ tablespoon coconut sugar

1 garlic clove

1 bay leaf

5 sprigs of thyme

salt and freshly ground black pepper

FOR THE CRISPY OYSTER MUSHROOMS

400 g (14 oz) oyster mushrooms

2 tablespoons Green Seasoning (see page 208)

1 tablespoon ground allspice

1 x quantity wet dredge (see page 124)

1 x quantity crispy coating (see page XX)

vegetable oil, for deep-frying

FOR THE SCOTCH BONNET BURNT LIME DRESSING

3 limes, halved

3 tablespoons soy sauce

1 Scotch bonnet, deseeded and chopped

1 garlic clove, finely diced

2 tablespoons light brown soft sugar

handful of coriander (cilantro) leaves

FOR THE SLAW

1 beetroot (beet), grated

1 carrot, grated

1 spring onion (scallion), finely chopped

2 tablespoons white wine vinegar

1 tablepsoon agave syrup

handful of roasted peanuts, roughly chopped

TO SERVE

sliced spring onions (scallions)

sliced red chili

Put the water, creamed coconut, sugar and plenty of salt into a saucepan. Be sure to really season it as this is the only opportunity you'll have to make sure the rice will be seasoned well. Add the rice, garlic clove, bay leaf and sprigs of thyme. Bring to the boil, then reduce the heat to low, cover and cook for 18–20 minutes. Remove from the heat and rest for a further 15–20 minutes.

Meanwhile, marinate the oyster mushrooms with the green seasoning and allspice. Allow to marinate for 20 minutes (this can also be done the day before).

Next, make the dressing. If you have a gas hob (stovetop), use tongs to hold the limes to the flame, flesh side down, until charred. If you don't have a gas hob, heat a little oil in a frying pan (skillet) over a medium high heat and fry the limes flesh side down until charred. Leave to cool a little, then squeeze the juice into a bowl and whisk in the remaining ingredients. Check for seasoning – it should be spicy, pokey and salty.

For the slaw, combine all the ingredients in a bowl and season to taste.

Put the ingredients for the wet dredge and crispy coating into two different bowls, seasoning the dry ingredients with plenty of salt and pepper.

Add a little of the wet dredge to the dry coating and mix in – this will create small lumps, which will become crispy pockets. Dip the mushrooms in the wet dredge, then into the coating mix and then repeat for a double coating. Tap off any excess coating and set aside on a baking sheet, ready to fry.

Pour enough vegetable oil into a high-sided heavy-bottomed frying pan (skillet) or saucepan to fill to halfway and gently bring to heat. Test the temperature by using a wooden spoon – if lots of bubbles appear around it immediately, it's ready to go.

Add 4–5 mushroom clusters to the pan, being careful not to overcrowd. Fry for 4–6 minutes until crisp. Drain off any excess oil on a wire rack. Repeat until all the mushrooms are cooked.

Serve the crispy mushrooms sprinkled with sliced chillies and spring onions, with the rice, dressing and slaw on the side so everyone can help themselves.

ACKEE SEASONED RICE

SERVES 4–6   PREP TIME : 5 MINUTES, PLUS 15 MINUTES RESTING TIME   COOK TIME : 30 MINUTES

This was my mother's fridge-raid dinner. Ackee would always be involved, but otherwise the ingredients changed according to what was available. Somehow, though, every rendition still felt like home.

This would be a great one to make for an unexpected guest, when you want to whip something up that you don't have to sit over so you can catch up with tea instead. In my mother's honour, I give you full permission to riff on this. Please add the veg that's on its last legs and whatever you have in the refrigerator ... Maybe you have some olives or sun-dried tomatoes hanging around? That would be lovely.

1 tablespoon olive oil

¾ teaspoon ground allspice

¾ teaspoon ground turmeric

¾ teaspoon ground cumin

1 onion, diced

2 red (bell) peppers, diced

1 garlic clove, very finely chopped

1 tablespoon chopped coriander (cilantro) stalks

300 g (10½ oz/1½ cups) jasmine or basmati rice, rinsed

400 ml (13 fl oz/generous 1½ cups) water

50 g (2 oz) creamed coconut

1 vegetable stock cube

200 g (7 oz) rinsed and drained ackee

salt and freshly ground black pepper to taste

Heat the olive oil in a heavy bottomed frying pan (skillet) or casserole dish (Dutch oven). Add the spices and toast for 1 minute, then add the onion with a pinch of salt and fry for 3–4 minutes until sweet and fragrant. Add the red peppers, garlic and chopped coriander stalks and fry for another minute.

Now add the rice and stir to coat with the oil and veggies. Add the water, creamed coconut, stock cube and ackee and season to taste with salt and pepper. Bring to the boil, then reduce the heat to low. Cover and allow to steam for 20 minutes, then remove from the heat and leave to sit, covered, for 10–15 minutes. It should be fluffy and full of flavour!

FOOD FOR COMPANY

JERK 'PORK' GYOZA

MAKES 12 GYOZA   PREP TIME : 20 MINUTES   COOK TIME : 5 MINUTES

Number 184,871,809 in the different ways of using jerk marinade! These gyoza are spicy, deeply savoury and easy to make. Make these for friends, or for yourself, like I did. They also freeze very well, so you can save any leftovers for future dumpling cravings.

250 g (9 oz) vegan minced (ground) pork

1 tablespoon soy sauce

1 tablespoon Dee's Classic Jerk Seasoning (see page 205)

¼ teaspoon ground allspice

2 cloves garlic, very finely shopped

3 large savoy cabbage leaves, chopped

2 spring onions (scallions), chopped

handful coriander (cilantro) leaves, chopped

1 packet of dumpling wrappers

1 tablespoon vegetable oil

80 ml (3 fl oz/⅓ cup) water

dipping sauces of your choice, to serve

Put the vegan minced pork into a bowl with the soy sauce, jerk seasoning, allspice, garlic, cabbage, spring onions and coriander. Mix well to combine.

Fill a small bowl with water and set out a baking sheet or plate dusted with a little flour or lined with cling film (plastic wrap). Take a dumpling wrapper and put a teaspoon of the filling in the middle, then use your finger to brush the edge with water. Close like a taco and then form the folds. Make sure it's sealed tight. Repeat to until all the filling is used up.

To cook the gyoza, heat the vegetable oil in a lidded frying pan (skillet) over a medium heat. Add some of the gyoza (making sure not to crowd the pan too much) and fry for about 2 minutes, or until golden brown underneath. Now add the water, cover and steam for 3–4 minutes until cooked through. Repeat to cook as many dumplings as you like, then serve with your favourite dipping sauce.

LYCHEE AND SCOTCH BONNET FROZEN MARG

SERVES 4   PREP TIME: 10 MINUTES, PLUS 4 HOURS FREEZING TIME   COOK TIME: 6 MINUTES

This is very much inspired by a bar in Margate, a town on the British coast, where I live. When I'm 'Margate tipsy', I'm referring to being three frozen margs deep at Little Swift on the seafront. It's that spicy-sweet combination that is just what I crave, even in a cocktail. The floral flavour of lychee just sings alongside the hot scotch bonnie. Make this for a girlfriend, or just for yourself. It's very much a treat and should be enjoyed in quantities.

565 g (20 oz) tin of lychees in syrup

1 Scotch bonnet, halved and deseeded

400 ml (13 fl oz/generous 1½ cups) lychee juice

bunch of mint leaves, plus extra to serve

200 ml (7 fl oz/scant 1 cup) tequila

100 ml (3½ fl oz/scant ½ cup) orange liqueur (such as Cointreau)

juice of 4 limes, plus extra for the glasses

2 handfuls of ice

TO SERVE

flaky salt

sliced limes

sliced chillies

SEE PHOTO OVERLEAF

Combine the syrup from the tin of lychees with the Scotch bonnet in a saucepan and set aside.

Transfer the lychees from the tin to a freezer-safe container and pour the lychee juice into an ice cube tray and freeze both for 4 hours.

Meanwhile, heat the lychee syrup and Scotch bonnet over a high heat for 5–6 minutes until reduced by half, then transfer the hot syrup to a jug (pitcher) and stir in the mint leaves. Leave to cool, then discard the Scotch bonnet.

Pour the cooled syrup into a food processor along with the remaining ingredients (including the frozen lychees and lychee juice) and blend to a slushy consistency.

Put some lime juice and flaky sea salt into two separate saucers or shallow dishes. Dip serving glasses in the lime juice first, followed by the flaky sea salt, then fill with the frozen marg and garnish with slices of lime, mint leaves and sliced chillies.

FOOD FOR COMPANY

SIDES THAT HAVE MAIN

EVENT ENERGY

Sides is a reductive term here, but I am here to proclaim that I am a side advocate. I am the type of person that orders three side dishes as a meal. Mainly because I'm deeply indecisive (Libra issues), but I think it's the perfect way to eat. Why just have a main dish when you can have thrice the number of interesting mouthfuls? When I started Dee's Table I always had the most fun creating the small plates on a menu. I'd spend a long time creating all the details and would have even more fun naming them!

Small plates give you more options when cooking for other people, as you can present a mini little spread of wonderful things to choose from. Generally speaking, you can break more rules with sides, and have the freedom to go off-script. When you think of sides, you're probably thinking veggies, which are not given as much respect as they should be, in my opinion. Vegetables deserve to be treated with main event energy – they are so exciting, but also flexible and interchangeable. Don't be afraid to char them beyond where you think they should go, and really give them the love and care you would any other dish or ingredient.

TRIBUTE TO HELLSHIRE

SERVES 4   PREP TIME: 15 MINUTES   COOK TIME: 20 MINUTES

I grew up eating fish and bammy (cassava flatbreads) at the seafood restaurants at Hellshire Beach, on the south coast of Jamaica. This tribute isn't fish and bammy, but it's bammy fried and coated in a nori salt, which gives you that ocean flavour. Most vegetables taste better charred and aubergine (eggplant) is a true testament to that. This aubergine dip is truly something special and paired with the bammy, it's a wonderful tribute indeed.

2 bammy, cut it into 6 pieces each

400ml (13 fl oz/generous 1½ cups) coconut milk

coconut oil, for frying

flaky sea salt

FOR THE SMOKY AUBERGINE DIP

1 aubergine

50 g (2 oz) tahini

1½ teaspoons smoked paprika

1 tablespoon tamarind paste

juice of 1 lemon

¾ teaspoon salt

freshly ground black pepper

FOR THE NORI SALT

2 nori sheets

2 dried porcini or shiitake mushrooms

1 teaspoon salt

½ teaspoon MSG

1 teaspoon garlic granules

1 teaspoon onion powder

Start by soaking the bammy. Combine the bammy with the coconut milk and a pinch or two of salt in a deep pan or bowl and leave to soak for 30 minutes.

Next, make the aubergine dip. Char the aubergine over an open flame on your hob (stovetop) for 10 minutes. Once charred, place in a bowl and cover with cling film (plastic wrap). Allow to sit for 5 minutes, then remove the charred skin and place the flesh in a food processor with the remaining ingredients. Blend until mostly smooth but with a few chunks.

To make the nori salt, put the nori sheets and mushrooms into a spice grinder or food processor and grind to a fine powder. Tip into a bowl and combine with the remaining ingredients.

Pat the bammy dry with paper towels and set aside. Melt enough coconut oil to coat in a frying pan (skillet) over a medium heat and fry the bammy pieces in batches for 3–4 minutes on each side until crispy. Transfer to a metal bowl and immediately hit with the nori salt, tossing to coat. Set aside on a wire rack.

Serve the dip in a bowl with the bammy placed around it.

CHEESE-STUFFED GARLIC AND SPRING ONION BREAD ROLLS

SERVES 6   PREP TIME: 40 MINUTES, PLUS 2½ HOURS PROVING TIME   COOK TIME: 20 MINUTES

I don't want to be dramatic, but if there's no bread for the table then can you
really call it a spread? Bread is my love language, especially when it's doused
with lots of garlic butter and spring onions (scallions). This one is for the garlic
lovers. Using both garlic granules and fresh garlic offers a deep savoury flavour.
These rolls are best served straight from the oven, but are also lovely the next
day for a breakfast sandwich.

85 g (3 oz) creamed coconut, chopped

200 ml (7 fl oz/scant 1 cup) soya milk

50 g (2 oz) vegan block butter,
plus extra for greasing

75 ml (2½ fl oz/5 tablespoons)
maple syrup

2 teaspoons active dry yeast

400 g (14 oz/scant 3¼ cups) strong white
bread flour

1 teaspoon salt

100 g (3½ oz) vegan sharp
Cheddar, cubed

3 spring onions (scallions),
finely chopped

olive oil, for greasing

FOR THE GARLIC BUTTER

50 g (2 oz) vegan block butter

4 garlic cloves, very finely chopped

1 teaspoon garlic granules

pinch of salt

In a saucepan, melt together the creamed coconut,
soya milk and butter over a low heat. Once melted,
remove from the heat and allow to cool until lukewarm.
Once cooled, add the maple syrup and yeast. Whisk and
then set aside for 5–6 minutes until foamy.

In the bowl of a stand mixer, combine the flour and salt.
Using the dough hook, mix on a low speed and slowly add
the wet ingredients to the dry. Turn it up to a medium
speed and knead for 7–8 minutes until elastic. The dough
should be a little sticky. Lightly oil a bowl and transfer
the dough to it. Cover with cling film (plastic wrap) and
leave to rise somewhere warm for 1½ hours, or until
doubled in size.

Once risen, punch down to remove the air from the dough
and tip out on a lightly floured surface, then divide the
dough into 12 balls.

Mix together the vegan cheese and spring onions in a bowl.
Place a ball of dough into the palm of your hand and fill
it with some of the cheese and spring onion mixture, rolling
to ensure they are well sealed. Repeat until all the balls
are filled.

Grease a deep 23 cm (9 inch) rectangular baking tray
(pan) with butter and place the balls in. Cover with cling
film and leave to rise again for 1 hour.

As the dough is rising, preheat the oven
to 180°C (400°F/gas 6).

Make the garlic butter by melting the butter in a saucepan
with the chopped garlic over a low-medium heat. Brown
very gently for 3–4 minutes until the garlic is toasty.
Stir in the garlic granules and salt, then set aside.

Once the buns have risen, brush with the garlic butter,
reserving a third for brushing once out of the oven.
Bake for 20 minutes until golden, then brush with
the remaining garlic butter and serve immediately.

LOADED TOSTONES WITH SPICY ROASTED CARROT DIP

SERVES 3–4   PREP TIME: 15 MINUTES   COOK TIME: 40 MINUTES

As a person who thrives on a good dip with a crispy dip-delivery vehicle, this recipe is the perfect marriage of crunchy, sour, spicy, garlicky and sweet! Carrots are the perfect vegetable for dips like this as they have a touch of sweetness that isn't too overwhelming. They're also such a great vehicle for spices and really love to be roasted. Served with crispy tostones, this is the perfect little snack or side dish to whip up for a late-afternoon vibe.

2 green plantains

olive oil, for frying

flaky sea salt

FOR THE SPICY ROASTED CARROT DIP

4 carrots, chopped

2 tablespoons olive oil, plus extra for roasting the carrots

1 tablespoon coriander seeds, roughly ground

1 tablespoon cumin seeds, roughly ground

1 teaspoon ground cinnamon

4 garlic cloves, unpeeled

170 g (6 oz) vegan cream cheese

50 g (2 oz) vegan-friendly kimchi

3 tablespoons kimchi juice

salt and freshly ground black pepper

Preheat the oven to 170°C (375°F/gas 5).

On a baking tray (pan), toss the carrots with a good glug of olive oil, the coriander seeds, cumin seeds, cinnamon and garlic cloves, and season with plenty of salt and pepper. Roast in the oven for 30 minutes until it's browned and caramelised.

Once cooked, transfer everything to a food processor (removing the skins from the garlic) and add the cream cheese, kimchi, kimchi juice and olive oil. Blend until smooth, then season to taste with salt and pepper. Transfer to a serving bowl.

Top and tail the green plantains and remove the peel by running a sharp knife along it and then peeling back to separate it from the flesh. Cut diagonally into 6–8 chunks.

In a frying pan (skillet), heat enough vegetable oil to coat the bottom of the pan over a medium-high heat. Fry the plantain slices for 3–4 minutes, flipping to cook on both sides. Remove and drain briefly paper towels, then transfer to a board and use a mug or bowl to flatten the pieces. Fry again for a further 2–3 minutes until crispy. Drain again on paper towels and hit immediately with some flaky sea salt.

Arrange the tostones around the dip on a serving plate to serve.

BRUSSEL SPROUTS WITH SCOTCH BONNET ROMESCO

SERVES 4   PREP TIME: 15 MINUTES   COOK TIME: 20 MINUTES

Brussels are finally getting the attention they deserve and I'm so happy
about it. Most vegetables taste infinitely better once charred and roasted,
but there's something very magical about roasted Brussels sprouts, as their
craggy, ribbon-like leaves allow for sauce to nestle in between them. People think
they dislike Brussels sprouts, but they're wrong. Most likely they have only had
them after they have been steamed to death. This recipe serves them alongside
a wonderfully pokey and warmly spiced romesco sauce, which they marry
with perfectly. This is the dish to convince all the Brussels haters you know.
Make this and change their minds.

500 g (1 lb 2 oz) sprouts, trimmed
and halved

2 tablespoons olive oil

½ teaspoon smoked paprika

2 tablespoons balsamic vinegar

2 teaspoons chopped thyme

salt and black pepper

FOR THE SCOTCH BONNET ROMESCO SAUCE

75 ml (2½ fl oz/5 tablespoons) olive oil

4 allspice berries (or 1 teaspoon
ground allspice)

6 cloves garlic (or more if you're into
your garlic)

1 Scotch bonnet, quartered (remove the
seeds if you prefer it to be less spicy)

50 g (2 oz/½ cup) flaked almonds
(or 30 g/1 oz blanched almonds),
plus extra to serve

3 roasted red peppers from a jar

4 tablespoons balsamic vinegar

100 g (3½ oz/3 tablespoons) stale bread
(any type), toasted and cubed

1 teaspoon salt

pinch of sugar

Preheat oven to 180°C (400°F/gas 6) and line a baking
tray (pan) with baking parchment.

Put the sprouts in a bowl and toss with the oil, paprika,
vinegar, thyme and some salt and pepper. Transfer
to the prepared baking tray and roast in the oven for
15–20 minutes until slightly charred.

For the romesco sauce, warm the olive oil in a small
saucepan over a medium heat. Add the allspice, garlic
cloves and scotch bonnet and allow to gently infuse for
8–10 minutes. A few minutes before the end, add the
almonds. Remove from the heat and set aside.

In a food processor, add the red peppers, balsamic
vinegar, bread, salt, pinch of sugar and the oil and almond
mixture. Blend into a slightly chunky texture, just before
being completely smooth.

Spoon some of the sauce onto a plate and top with the
charred sprouts, then garnish with more almond flakes.
Store the remaining sauce in an airtight container for
up to 1 week. It's so delish on so many other dishes.

SPRING VEG RUNDOWN

SERVES 3–4   PREP TIME : 10 MINUTES   COOK TIME : 20 MINUTES

Spring is my favourite season. I am no longer an autumn (fall) girl – that is the old me. Entering spring after a long winter feels like literal hope to me. Spring produce is also the best, with so much to offer. Strawb season begins and sweet and waxy new potatoes come into our lives, but most importantly, asparagus season reigns. Rundown is a stew, typically made with salted or cured mackerel. I have replaced them here with preserved artichokes, which I adore. The spring veg is asparagus and chard, which are added near to the end of cooking to retain their flavour. Although this recipe is dedicated to spring, feel free to make up a winter rundown with leeks and squash.

2 tablespoons olive oil

1 onion, diced

1 tablespoons allspice berries

½ Scotch bonnet, deseeded and finely chopped

2 spring onions (scallions), finely sliced

1 small tomato, diced

1 red (bell) pepper, sliced

4 garlic cloves, very finely chopped

1 vegetable stock cube dissolved in 200 ml (7 fl oz/scant 1 cup) boiling water

140 g (4¾ oz) chargrilled artichokes from a jar, quartered

400 ml (13 fl oz/generous 1½ cups) coconut milk

1 bay leaf

3 sprigs of thyme

250 g (9 oz) asparagus spears, cut into threes

200 g (7 oz) Swiss chard, sliced

juice of ¼ lemon

salt and freshly ground black pepper

Heat the oil in a frying pan (skillet) over a medium high heat and fry the onion with a pinch of salt for 4–5 minutes until softened. Add the allspice berries, Scotch bonnet, spring onions and tomato and fry for 2 minutes until fragrant and the tomatoes are a little softened. Add the red pepper and garlic and cook for 2 minutes more.

Deglaze the pan with the stock, scraping up any brown bits. Add the artichokes, coconut milk, bay leaf and sprigs of thyme. Bring to the boil, then reduce the heat to a simmer, add the asparagus and chard and wilt for 4–5 minutes with the lid on. Season with salt and pepper and then brighten the flavours with a squeeze of the lemon.

STICKY HISPI CABBAGE WITH CRISPY SHALLOTS

SERVES 3–4   PREP TIME: 10 MINUTES   COOK TIME: 30 MINUTES

Hispi cabbage is such a humble ingredient. I grew up absolutely loving cabbage as a really simple and quick meal. My mother used to steam it with LOTS of garlic and soy sauce and top it with fried onions. This recipe involves pan-frying it in brown butter and then coating it with a sorrel hoisin sauce, which makes it feel really special. The cabbage leaves get lovely and glazed and slightly crispy in all the right places.

2 tablespoons vegan block butter

1 hispi (sweetheart) cabbage, halved lengthways

2 garlic cloves

splash of vegetable stock

1 x quantity Sorrel Hoisin Glaze (see page 209)

1 sliced red chilli

handful of crispy shallots

salt

Preheat the oven to 170°C (375°F/gas 5).

Heat the butter in a lidded, ovenproof frying pan (skillet) over a medium heat until foamy, then add the cabbage cut side down. Press into the frying pan and caramelise for 4–5 minutes. Once lovely and caramelised, flip over, add the garlic cloves, season with salt and baste with the brown butter. Add a splash of vegetable stock, cover and steam for 5–6 minutes until just cooked through.

Glaze with some of the sorrel hoisin, then transfer to the oven and roast for 15 minutes until caramelised.

To serve, spread a little of the sorrel hoisin over the base of a serving dish and add the cabbage on top. Garnish with the chilli and crispy shallots.

JAMMY SHALLOTS IN A POKEY TOMATO SAUCE

SERVES 4   PREP TIME : 15 MINUTES   COOK TIME : 30 MINUTES

Sun-dried tomatoes are a punchy flavour bomb, salty and sweet, and my love
for shallots is undeniable. Far sweeter and jammier than their counterpart,
I'll always reach for them over regular onions. I really enjoy tomatoes and onions,
a classic pairing, but this feels like it's cool cousin. This side could be a great
starter (appetizer), served with frozen parathas (of course) for scooping
up all the goodness!

4 tablespoons sun-dried tomato oil

6–10 shallots, halved if large

1 teaspoon fennel seeds

1 teaspoon coriander seeds

1 teaspoon ground allspice

1 tablespoon tomato purée (paste)

½ Scotch bonnet, deseeded and chopped

1 tablespoon soy sauce

1 tablespoon balsamic vinegar

1 tablespoon light brown soft sugar

4 tablespoons water

8 garlic cloves, lightly smashed

thick dairy-free yoghurt, to serve

6 tablespoons sun-dried tomatoes, chopped

parathas, to serve

Preheat the oven to 180°C (400°F/gas 6).

Heat the sun-dried tomato oil in an ovenproof frying
pan (skillet) over a medium-high heat and add the
shallots, cut side down. Brown for 5 minutes without
moving them. Meanwhile, grind the spices together in a
spice grinder or mortar and pestle. Remove the shallots
from the pan and add the tomato purée, Scotch bonnet
and spices. Allow to cook out in the oil for 2–3 minutes,
until the tomato paste has darkened.

In a small bowl, mix together the soy sauce, balsamic
vinegar, brown sugar and water. Add this to the pan to
deglaze it, then add the shallots back to the pan, cut side
down, along with the garlic cloves. Transfer to the oven
and roast for 20 minutes until the shallots are sticky and
wonderfully glazed.

To serve, spread a serving dish with yoghurt and then
top with the shallots. Drizzle over any remaining sauce
from the pan and garnish with the chopped sun-dried
tomatoes. Scoop up with some fried frozen parathas!

ROASTED SQUASH IN SUN-DRIED TOMATO OIL

SERVES 6   PREP TIME : 5 MINUTES   COOK TIME : 40 MINUTES

Never throw away the oil from a jar of sun-dried tomatoes. They are loaded with flavour, and the longer you have had them, the deeper that flavour gets. Red kuri squash is my favourite – super creamy, waxy and slightly starchier than the other squashes. In my opinion it holds up well to the the sun-dried tomato oil.

1 red kuri squash, cut into thick wedges

2 shallots, halved

6 garlic cloves, unpeeled

4 tablespoons sun-dried tomato oil

1 teaspoon coriander seeds

1 teaspoon ground cinnamon

salt and freshly ground black pepper

non-dairy Greek-style yoghurt, to serve

handful of flat-leaf parsley leaves, roughly chopped, to serve

roti or paratha, to serve

Preheat the oven to 180°C (400°F/gas 6).

On a baking tray (pan), toss the squash, shallots and garlic with the sun-dried tomato oil, coriander seeds and cinnamon and season with salt and pepper. Roast in the oven for 40 minutes, flipping the squash after 25 minutes.

Spread some yoghurt on a serving dish and and top with the squash, shallot and roasted garlic. Add the parsley on top and serve with roti or frozen paratha to mop everything up.

SIDES THAT HAVE MAIN EVENT ENERGY

ROASTED CORN AND
SPRING ONION GRATIN

SERVES 4–6   PREP TIME : 10 MINUTES   COOK TIME : 30 MINUTES

Corn and spring onions (scallions) go hand in hand for me. A marriage that can never be separated. This recipe feels like a BBQ kind of side dish as the charred corn flavour and smell just sing charcoal heaven.

3 corn on the cob

5 spring onions (scallions), finely chopped

30 g (1 oz/¼ cup) gram (chickpea) flour

250 ml (8½ fl oz/1 cup) non-dairy double (heavy) cream

½ teaspoon salt

1 tablespoon olive oil

2 tablespoons polenta (cornmeal)

1 teaspoon garlic granules

1 tablespoon nutritional yeast

50 g (2 oz) vegan Cheddar, grated, plus extra for topping

vegan butter, for greasing

freshly ground black pepper

Preheat the oven to 180°C (400°F/gas 6).

Start by charring the corn. If you have a gas hob (stovetop), you can do this directly over the flame until the cobs are evenly charred on each side. Otherwise, char the corn in a frying pan (skillet) with a little oil over a medium heat, rotating until the cobs are evenly blistered. Once the corn is charred, remove from the heat and use a sharp knife to remove the kernels from the cob. Transfer to a bowl and set aside.

In a separate bowl, combine all the remaining ingredients except the cheese and season with lots of black pepper. Mix well until smooth. Add the corn and the cheese and stir to combine.

Grease a cast-iron frying pan with vegan butter, then pour in the corn mixture. Finally, sprinkle over some more cheese and bake in the oven for 20 minutes until golden and crispy on top.

SILKY BUTTER BEANS WITH ROASTED CORN AND HAZELNUTS

SERVES 4–6   PREP TIME : 15 MINUTES   COOK TIME : 30 MINUTES

There are no secrets or tricks here. Just a humble bowl of beans with wonderful sweet and crunchy bits. The base starts with olive oil, onions and whole garlic cloves that ooze a more subtle flavour into the pan. Beans can go a long way. They're cheap, creamy and with a bit of care can be transformed into a glorious meal. They work so well in quick braises like this and soak up so much flavour.

50 g (2 oz/scant ⅓ cup) hazelnuts

1 onion, finely diced

4 garlic cloves, smashed

2 x 400 g (14 oz) tins of butter (lima) beans, rinsed and drained

4 sprigs of thyme

1 bay leaf

1 vegetable stock cube dissolved in 350 ml (12 fl oz/1½ cups) boiling water

1 corn on the cob

splash of apple cider vinegar

olive oil, for frying

roughly chopped flat-leaf parsley leaves, to garnish

Preheat the oven to 170°C (375°F/gas 5).

Spread the hazelnuts out on a baking sheet and toast in the oven for 10–15 minutes until well browned. Remove from the oven and allow to cool.

Meanwhile, heat a generous amount of olive oil in a frying pan (skillet) over a medium heat. This is also a part of the flavour, so do be generous! Add the onion with a good pinch of salt and sweat for 2–3 minutes until fragrant nd softened, then add the smashed whole garlic cloves. Fry until fragrant, then add the beans and coat in the oil for a few minutes. Next, add the thyme, bay leaf and stock. Bring to the boil, then cover and simmer for 20 minutes until the sauce has thickened.

Meanwhile, char the corn. If you have a gas hob (stovetop), use tongs to hold the corn over the flame until charred. If you don't have a gas hob, heat a little oil in a frying pan over a medium-high heat and fry until charred. Use a sharp knife to shave the kernels from the cob and set aside.

Check the beans for seasoning and then add a splash of apple cider vinegar. Using the back of a fork, smush some of the butter beans in the pan to create a lush texture. Spoon the beans onto a serving dish, sprinkle the corn over the top and then add the hazelnuts. Top with some parsley to finish.

SIDES THAT HAVE MAIN EVENT ENERGY

SWEET AND STICKY JERK CARROTS WITH FETA

SERVES 4–6   PREP TIME : 5 MINUTES   COOK TIME : 45 MINUTES

Carrots stand up well to quite aggressive spicing, and they really deepen in colour and change texture when roasted. In this dish I use my jerk seasoning, which is a wonderful blend of earthy spices. It's really lovely as a sweet glaze with the salty and creamy texture of the vegan feta cheese. I'm a big fan of sweet and salty flavours in the same dish. This feels like it could be a good weekday dinner with a couple of other sides.

8 carrots, halved lengthways

1 teaspoon garlic granules

1 teaspoon ground allspice

2 tablespoons Dee's Classic Jerk Seasoning (see page 205)

2 tablespoons agave syrup

100 g (3½ oz) vegan feta, crumbled

handful of flat-leaf parsley leaves, roughly chopped

olive oil, for roasting the carrots

salt and freshly ground black pepper

Preheat the oven to 180°C (400°F/gas 6).

In a baking tray (pan), toss the carrots with the garlic granules, allspice, a glug of olive oil and some salt and pepper. Roast in the oven for 30 minutes.

In a small bowl, whisk together the jerk seasoning and agave syrup. After 30 minutes, take the carrots out of the oven and add the jerk and agave mixture. Stir to coat the carrots evenly, then return to the oven to bake for a further 15 minutes until caramelised.

Once cooked, transfer to a serving plate and sprinkle over the feta and parsley.

ROASTED CAULIFLOWER WITH SULTANAS AND PECAN BROWN BUTTER

SERVES 2–3   PREP TIME : 30 MINUTES   COOK TIME : 35 MINUTES

Roasting is one of my favourite ways to eat cauliflower. It becomes nutty and slightly sweet in the process. This cauliflower is lightly spiced and it works so wonderfully with the pecans and brown butter.

1 cauliflower, separated into florets

1 tablespoon ground coriander

1 tablespoon garlic granules

1 teaspoon cinnamon

1 teaspoon ground allspice

100 g (3½ oz/generous ¾ cup) sultanas (golden raisins)

juice of 2 lemons

50 g (2 oz) vegan block butter

50 g (2 oz/½ cup) pecans

1 garlic clove, very finely chopped

olive oil, for roasting

salt and freshly ground black pepper

roughly chopped flat-leaf parsley leaves, to garnish

Preheat the oven to 170°C (375°F/gas 5).

Put the cauliflower onto a baking tray (pan), drizzle with olive oil, then sprinkle over the ground coriander, garlic granules, cinnamon and allspice. Season to taste with salt and pepper, toss to coat, then roast in the oven for 30 minutes, or until caramelised.

Meanwhile, soak the sultanas in the white wine vinegar until tender.

Heat the butter in a frying pan (skillet) over a medium heat. Add the pecans and brown for 4–5 minutes, then add the garlic and immediately remove from the heat. Season with salt and pepper.

Arrange the roasted cauliflower over the base of a dish and dress with the browned pecan butter and sprinkle with parsley. Finally scatter the golden raisins around the dish.

NEW POTATOES WITH HERBY CREMA AND CASHEW CHILLI NORI OIL

SERVES 4-6   PREP TIME : 25 MINUTES   COOK TIME : 45 MINUTES

This side is bold and punchy and has lots of lovely textures through it. New potatoes are perfect for smashing as they are waxy, so they hold their shape. As you will have discovered by now, I love nori and I will not stop until I've found a way to introduce it into most dishes.

SIDES THAT HAVE MAIN EVENT ENERGY

750 g (1 lb 10 oz) new potatoes

olive oil, for roasting

salt

FOR THE HERBY CREMA

bunch of flat-leaf parsley, leaves picked

bunch of coriander (cilantro), leaves picked

300 g (10½ oz) silken tofu

1 garlic clove

juice of 1 lemon

salt and freshly ground black pepper

FOR THE CASHEW CHILLI NORI OIL

2 nori sheets

120 ml (4 fl oz/½ cup) olive oil

70 g (2¼ oz/scant ½ cup) cashews, roughly chopped

1 Scotch bonnet, finely sliced

3 garlic cloves

zest of 2 limes

1 tablespoon maple syrup

1 teaspoon salt

Preheat the oven to 180°C (400°F/gas 6).

Put the new potatoes in a saucepan, cover with cold water and season liberally with salt. It should taste like the sea. Bring to the boil, then cook for about 15 minutes until fork tender. Drain, transfer to a baking tray (pan) and drizzle with olive oil. Season with salt and pepper and crush with a mug. Roast in the oven for 30 minutes until crispy.

Meanwhile, make the crema. Blend all the ingredients in a high-speed blender until smooth. Set aside.

Next make the chilli oil. Grind the nori sheet sheets into a powder using a spice grinder or blender.

In a small saucepan, heat the olive oil over a medium heat, add the cashews and stir for 30 seconds until golden brown. Add the chilli and nori, stir and toast for another 30 seconds. Remove from the heat and add the garlic cloves and lime zest, then stir and allow the residual heat to cook the garlic. Add the maple syrup and salt, stir, then transfer to a clean jar.

Spread a good dollop of the crema over the base of a serving plate. Top with the smashed potatoes, then dress with the cashew chilli nori oil.

DESSERT AS A

LiFE STYLE

A bad dessert can ruin a meal, while a great dessert will live on in your memory forever. I find people are very particular when it comes to desserts. Chocolate lovers, fruit enthusiasts, vanilla and nutty girls (me). And then there are the cheese board fans, who I have a lot of respect for. However, let's get things straight. A cheese board is a snack, not a dessert. This chapter is called 'dessert as a lifestyle' because I will never not have a dessert, it's not even a question for me. I'm the kind of person that needs mini desserts after each meal to keep me going. I will only opt out of dessert when I'm dining out and the only vegan dessert option is a fruit-based sorbet, then I will not order it out of protest.

My dessert cravings are weather dependent. There is something wonderful about eating pavlova on a warm summer evening, or about a late-afternoon slice of dense loaf cake when it's raining outside, serving as the perfect accompaniment to a good book and a pot of tea. This chapter demonstrates my dessert preferences. I love big flavours. I want my pudding to be bursting with the flavour it should be.

SWEETCORN PANNA COTTA

SERVES 4   PREP TIME : 15 MINUTES, PLUS 6 HOURS CHILLING TIME   COOK TIME : 7 MINUTES

Growing up, my mother would eat sweetcorn with condensed milk and
cream or milk for a quick and easy dessert. It's such a simple combination,
but it brings back so many memories. Panna cotta is my go-to dessert order
if I see it on a menu. No bells and whistles, just bursting with vanilla flavour
and served with something fruity.

1 tablespoon vegan block butter

150 g (5 oz/1 cup) sweetcorn (tinned, frozen or fresh)

250 ml (8½ fl oz/1 cup) non-dairy double (heavy) cream

400 ml (13 fl oz/generous 1½ cups) coconut milk

100 ml (3½ fl oz/scant ½ cup) non-dairy condensed milk

1 tablespoon vanilla paste or 1 vanilla pod (bean), split and seeds scraped out

1 teaspoon agar-agar

50 g (2 oz) plain non-dairy yoghurt

2 tablespoons cornflour (cornstarch)

toffee popcorn, to serve

freshly grated nutmeg, to serve

Melt the butter in a frying pan (skillet) over a medium
heat. Add the sweetcorn and allow to caramelise for
3–4 minutes until slightly browned.

Transfer the butter and sweetcorn to a food processor
and add the cream, coconut milk, condensed milk,
vanilla and agar-agar. Blend until completely smooth.

Transfer the mixture to a saucepan and bring to a gentle
boil, then cook for 2–3 minutes over a medium heat,
stirring continuously. It should thicken slightly. Remove
from the heat.

Temper the yoghurt by adding a little of the hot sweetcorn
cream and stirring to combine. Add this to the pan with
the rest of the sweetcorn cream, stir to combine and
then blend again. Pass through a sieve and then divide
between six ramekins. Leave to cool for 30 minutes
at room temperature, then refrigerate for 4–6 hours
until completely set.

To serve, either top straightaway with toffee popcorn
and grated nutmeg, or dip each ramekin into hot water
to loosen and turn over onto a serving plate.

NO-CHURN RUM AND RAISIN ICE CREAM

SERVES 4–6   PREP TIME : 10 MINUTES, PLUS OVERNIGHT SOAKING AND 4 HOURS FREEZING TIME
COOK TIME : 3 MINUTES

Rum and raisin was always my go-to ice cream flavour. It was the flavour
everyone in my family could settle on in the supermarket – and it's what I have
missed so deeply since going vegan! No-churn ice creams are just so easy to put
together, they are the perfect carefree dessert to make for a low-key dinner.

100 ml (3½ fl oz/scant ½ cup) dark rum

80 g (3 oz/scant ¾ cup) raisins

250 ml (8½ fl oz/1 cup) non-dairy double
(heavy) cream

150 ml (5 fl oz/scant ⅔ cup) non-dairy
condensed milk

1 tablespoon vanilla extract or paste

Heat the rum in a saucepan over a medium heat until it's
just hot – not boiling. Pour over the raisins in a small bowl
and leave to soak overnight.

The next day, whisk the cream in a bowl to firm,
soft peaks. Add the condensed milk and vanilla extract
to the soaked raisins, then fold them into the cream.
Pour the mixture into a metal loaf tin (pan) or ice cream
tub and cover with a lid or cling film (plastic wrap). Freeze
for 3–4 hours until set.

DESSERT AS A LIFESTYLE

SIMPLE ORANGE AND YOGHURT CORNMEAL LOAF

SERVES 8–10   PREP TIME: 20 MINUTES, PLUS 1 HOUR RESTING TIME   COOK TIME: 1 HOUR 5 MINUTES

Sometimes you simply just need cake. In fact, I would like this cake right now. It's worth the wait – giving the cake enough time to soak up the syrup takes it to another level. This orange and yoghurt loaf comes together with such simple ingredients, doesn't require any special equipment and the polenta (cornmeal) adds a wonderful texture to the crumb. The use of olive oil and yoghurt keeps the cake very moist.

300 g (10½ oz/generous 2⅓ cups) plain (all-purpose) flour

100 g (3½ oz/⅔ cup) polenta (cornmeal)

1½ teaspoons baking powder

½ teaspoon bicarbonate of soda (baking soda)

250 g (9 oz) plain non-dairy yoghurt

150 ml (5 fl oz/scant ⅔ cup) non-dairy milk

100 ml (3½ fl oz/scant ½ cup) olive oil, plus extra for greasing

150 g (5 oz/generous ¾ cup) light brown soft sugar

1 tablespoon vanilla extract

zest of 4 oranges

1 teaspoon orange extract

FOR THE ORANGE SYRUP

juice of 4 oranges

100 ml (3½ fl oz/scant ½ cup) agave syrup

Preheat the oven to 160°C (350°F/gas 4). Grease a 900 g (2 lb/9 x 5 x 3 inch) loaf tin (pan) and line with baking parchment lengthways with the paper overhanging the ends of the tin, so that the cake will be easy to remove once baked.

Combine the flour, polenta, baking powder and bicarbonate of soda in a large bowl. In a separate bowl, mix together the yoghurt, milk, oil, sugar, vanilla extract, orange zest and orange extract. Now add the wet mixture to the dry and fold in until it just comes together. Pour the cake batter into the prepared tin and smooth out the top.

Bake in the oven for 50–55 minutes until a skewer inserted into the centre comes out clean. Leave to cool in the tin for 10 minutes while you prepare the syrup.

Combine the orange juice and the agave syrup in a saucepan. Bring to the boil and bubble for 6–8 minutes until reduced by half. Using a skewer, poke holes in the top of the cake for the syrup. Pour the syrup over the cake and swirl it around until it soaks through. Rest for 45–60 minutes before slicing.

COCONUT GIZZADA STREUSEL LOAF

SERVES 8   PREP TIME : 20 MINUTES, PLUS 30 MINUTES RESTING TIME   COOK TIME : 1¼ HOURS

Coconut Gizzada is a very popular Jamaican snack consisting of a pastry case (shell) filled with a mixture of coconut, brown sugar and spices. I love it, so I decided to make it into cake form, inspired by old-fashioned coffee cakes with a streusel running through it. This loaf is impossibly fluffy and each part of the cake is flooded with coconut flavour. It is a perfect lazy Saturday afternoon bake with your siblings or friends.

60 g (2 oz/⅔ cup) desiccated (dried shredded) coconut

250 g (9 oz/2 cups) plain (all-purpose) flour

¼ teaspoon salt

1 teaspoon baking powder

½ teaspoon bicarbonate of soda (baking soda)

½ teaspoon ground cinnamon

70 g (2¼ oz) silken tofu

200 ml (7 fl oz/scant 1 cup) soya milk

80 g (3 oz) creamed coconut

1½ teaspoons vanilla extract

115 g (4 oz/½ cup) coconut oil

115 g (4 o/½ cup) caster (superfine) sugar

FOR THE CARAMEL

50 g (2 oz/generous ¼ cup) soft brown sugar

30 g (1 oz/½ cup) toasted coconut

¼ teaspoon salt

FOR THE STREUSEL

50 g (2 oz/scant ½ cup) plain flour

50 g (2 oz/generous ¼ cup) light brown soft sugar

50 g (2 oz) vegan block butter, plus extra for greasing

30 g (1 oz/½ cup) toasted coconut

¼ teaspoon salt

½ teaspoon ground cinnamon

Preheat the oven to 170°C (375°F/gas 5). Grease a 900 g (2 lb/9 x 5 x 3 inch) loaf tin (pan) with butter and line lengthways with baking parchment, with the paper overhanging the ends of the tin, so that the cake will be easy to remove once baked.

Heat a dry frying pan (skillet) over a medium-low heat and toast the desiccated coconut for 3–4 minutes until evenly browned. Transfer to a bowl and allow to cool.

Sift the flour, salt, baking powder, bicarbonate of soda and cinnamon into a large bowl and stir to combine.

In a separate bowl or blender, whisk together the silken tofu, soya milk, creamed coconut and vanilla, then transfer to a saucepan. Simmer on a low heat, then add the coconut oil and let it melt into the mixture. Add the sugar and whisk until combined. Gently fold in the dry ingredients and mix until smooth. Set aside.

In a small bowl, mix together the ingredients for the caramel.

For the streusel, combine all ingredients in a bowl and rub the butter into the dry ingredients until the mixture resembles breadcrumbs.

To assemble, pour half of the batter into the prepared tin, then add the caramel mixture, then the rest of the batter, and finally top with the streusel mixture.

Bake for 60 minutes, covering with kitchen foil if the top starts to get too brown. Leave to cool in the tin for 30 minutes before turning out and cutting.

DESSERT AS A LIFESTYLE

JAMAICAN GINGER
AND MARZIPAN LOAF

SERVES 8–10   PREP TIME : 25 MINUTES, PLUS 30 MINUTES RESTING TIME   COOK TIME : 1¼ HOURS

My favourite cakes to make are oil-based loaf cakes. They're foolproof – always moist and never dry. So it made sense to create a ginger and marzipan loaf cake, one of my dream flavour combinations. Anything with a deep almondy flavour is a win for me. Sticky ginger cake, both fiery and deeply sweet – perfect.

DESSERT AS A LIFESTYLE

230 g (8¼ oz) marzipan

250 g (9 oz/2 cups) plain (all-purpose) lour

2 tablespoons ground ginger

1 teaspoon ground cinnamon

1 teaspoon bicarbonate of soda (baking soda)

1 teaspoon baking powder

¼ teaspoon salt

70 g (2¼ oz) silken tofu

200 ml (7 fl oz/scant 1 cup) non-dairy milk

90 g (3¼ oz/¼ cup) black treacle (molasses)

90 g (3¼ oz/¼ cup) golden (light corn) syrup

90 g (3¼ oz/scant ½ cup) dark brown soft sugar

130 g (4½ oz) vegan block butter, plus extra for greasing

1 tablespoon water

1 teaspoon vanilla extract

1½ teaspoons almond extract

zest of 2 limes

non-dairy vanilla ice cream or créme fraîche

Preheat the oven to 170°C (375°F/gas 5). Grease a 900 g (2 lb/9 x 5 x 3 inch) loaf tin (pan) and line with baking parchment, with the paper ovehanging the ends of the tin, so that the cake will be easy to remove once baked.

Grate 150 g (5 oz) of the marzipan and chop the remaining 80 g (3 oz) into chunks. Toss both the grated marzipan and the chunks with 2 tablespoons of the flour and set aside.

Sift the flour, ginger, cinnamon, bicarbonate soda, baking powder and salt into a large bowl and whisk to combine.

Blend or whisk together the silken tofu and milk together and set aside.

Combine the treacle, golden syrup, sugar, butter and water in a saucepan over a medium-low heat and gently cook until the butter has just melted and the sugar has dissolved, making sure it doesn't boil. Then stir in the vanilla extract, almond extract, lime zest and the blended tofu and milk mixture. Mix to combine.

Add the wet mixture to the dry, whisking until smooth, then stir in the marzipan. Pour the batter into the prepared tin.

Bake in the oven for 1 hour 5 minutes until a skewer inserted into the centre comes out clean. Leave to cool in the tin for 30 minutes before turning out and slicing and serving with ice cream or créme fraîche.

PASSION FRUIT GLAZED DOUGHNUTS

MAKES 10 DOUGHNUTS   PREP TIME: 40 MINUTES, PLUS 2½ HOURS PROVING TIME
COOK TIME: 20 MINUTES

A glazed doughnut heals a lot of things internally for me. Something that a cookie or even a really nice slice of cake will never do. I'll take a well-made doughnut over one of their baking treat competitors any day (hides face). OK, let's talk about it. Actually, no, I will FIGHT you on this. You can't change my mind.

For doughnuts, I think the simpler the flavour the better. These passionfruit ring doughnuts feel simple and slightly fancy at the same time. They're not something you make all the time, so you might as well add some passion fruit into the mix and indulge your fried dough cravings. You are welcome.

70 g (2¼ oz) silken tofu

250 ml (8½ fl oz/1 cup) soya milk

45 g (1¾ oz) vegan block butter

2 teaspoons vanilla extract

2½ teaspoons active dry yeast

400 g (14 oz/scant 3¼ cups) strong white bread flour

45 g (1¾ oz/scant ¼ cup) white cane sugar

¼ teaspoon salt

vegetable oil, for greasing and frying

FOR THE GLAZE

juice and seeds of 2 passion fruit

zest of 1 lime

100 g (3½ oz/generous ¾ cup) icing (confectioners' sugar)

1 teaspoon vanilla extract

pinch of salt

Blending or whisk together the tofu and milk, then transfer to a saucepan with the butter and vanilla extract. Gently heat until the butter is completely melted, taking care not to let it boil. Transfer to a jug (pitcher) to cool until lukewarm, then mix in the yeast. Leave to activate for 5–6 minutes until foamy.

Combine the flour, sugar and salt in the bowl of a stand mixer. Mix using the dough hook to combine, then gently stream in the yeast mixture and knead on a medium speed for 8–10 minutes. The dough should be a little sticky but spring back slightly when you touch it. Lightly oil a bowl and transfer the dough to it. Cover with cling film (plastic wrap) and leave to rise somewhere warm for 1½ hours, or until doubled in size (1).

Once risen, punch down to release the air from the dough and tip out on a lightly floured surface. Roll out the dough to about 1 cm (½ inch) thick (2). Cut out as many doughnuts as you can using a 10 cm (4 inch) and a 2.5 cm (1 inch) cookie cutter (3). Reform the dough, roll out again and cut more doughnuts (always keep the doughnut holes). Transfer the doughnuts to a lightly floured baking sheet, cover with cling film and leave to rise for another 1 hour until doubled in size again.

→

Pour enough vegetable oil into a high-sided heavy-bottomed frying pan (skillet) or saucepan to fill it halfway and gently bring to heat. Test the temperature by using a wooden spoon – if lots of bubbles appear around it immediately, it's ready to go. Fry the doughnuts in batches for 2–3 minutes on each side until golden. Drain on paper towels. Once all the doughnuts are fried allow to cool for 20–30 minutes.

Meanwhile, make the glaze by whisking together all the ingredients. It should be the consistency of double (heavy) cream.

Dip each cooled doughnut into the glaze (4) and then transfer to a wire rack placed over a baking sheet to harden before eating.

1

2

3

4

DARK CHOCOLATE AND PECAN COFFEE CARAMEL TART

SERVES 6   PREP TIME : 30 MINUTES, PLUS 3 HOURS CHILLING TIME   COOK TIME : 25 MINUTES

A pecan-flavoured dessert is right up there for me and paired with dark chocolate it really hits the mark. The base is baked, but the rest of it comes together really quickly and just needs to chill in the refrigerator to set.

FOR THE PECAN CARAMEL

1 tablespoon instant coffee or instant espresso powder

60 ml (2 fl oz/¼ cup) boiling water

115–125 g (3¾–4 oz) coconut cream

1 teaspoon vanilla extract

90 g (3¼ oz/scant ½ cup) dark brown soft sugar

¼ teaspoon salt

150 g (5 oz/1½ cups) pecans, plus extra to decorate

FOR THE BASE

300 g (10½ oz) Biscoff biscuits (cookies)

100 g (3½ oz) vegan block butter, melted, plus extra for greasing

FOR THE CHOCOLATE FILLING

400 ml (13 fl oz/generous 1½ cups) coconut milk

2 tablespoons agave syrup

300 g (10½ oz) 70% dark (bittersweet) vegan chocolate, roughly chopped

1 tablespoon vanilla extract

50g (¼ cup) coconut yogurt

flaky sea salt, to decorate

Preheat the oven to 160°C (350°F/gas 4). Grease a 23 cm (9 inch) loose-bottomed tart tin and line the base with a ring of baking parchment.

First, make the caramel. In a small saucepan, dissolve the coffee or espresso powder in the boiling water. Add the coconut cream, vanilla extract, sugar and salt and mix together, then bring to the boil and allow to bubble, stirring constantly, for 5–6 minutes until reduced by half. Pour into a bowl and allow to cool.

In a food processor or using a ziplock bag and a rolling pan, blitz or bash the biscuits into a fine powder. Transfer to a bowl and add the melted butter. Mix together with your hands – it should just come together when you squeeze it.

Place half of the biscuit base mixture into the tin and form the edge, then place the rest in the middle and form the base. Even it out with the bottom of a cup or glass.

Place the tin on a baking sheet and scatter the pecans next to it on the sheet to toast as the base is baking. Bake in the oven for 15 minutes.

Next, make the chocolate filling. Warm the coconut milk with the agave syrup in a saucepan over a medium heat until steaming. Put the chocolate into a bowl and pour over the hot coconut milk. Mix with a spatula until the chocolate has melted. Add the vanilla extract and stir to combine. Allow to cool for a few minutes, then fold in the yoghurt.

To assemble, pour the caramel into the prepared base, then break up the roasted pecans with your hands and scatter over the caramel. Pour over the chocolate filling and even out with a palette knife or spatula. Top with more pecans and a pinch of flaky sea salt. Leave to sit in the refrigerator for at least 3 hours before serving.

PINEAPPLE, MINT AND BROWN BUTTER ALMOND CAKE

SERVES 6–8   PREP TIME: 25 MINUTES   COOK TIME: 1 HOUR

There's very, very few things that brown butter won't improve. It deepens and complements the sweet and floral qualities of pineapple and mint in this cake. As you'll know by now, I'm not heavy on the iced (frosted) cakes. I tend to veer towards cakes that are based on some kind of nut or fruit, and which require very little decorative skills. I imagine this cake would be a great spring dinner party cake, something to take to a friend's house to impress everyone. Also, it's gluten free! So you get to say, 'BTW this is gluten free' and then bask in all the praise for your wizardry.

100 g (3½ oz) vegan block butter, plus extra for greasing

aquafaba from 1 x 400 g (14 oz) tin of chickpeas

1 teaspoon cream of tartar

pinch of salt

100 g (3½ oz/generous ½ cup) light brown soft sugar

50 ml (1 ¾ fl oz/3 tablespoons) soya milk

1 teaspoon vanilla extract

1 teaspoon almond extract

235 g (8¼ oz/2⅓ cups) ground almonds (almond meal)

100 g (3½ oz/generous ¾ cup) gluten-free plain (all-purpose) flour

¾ teaspoon baking powder

FOR THE MUDDLED PINEAPPLE

350 g (12 oz) fresh pineapple, chopped

2 passion fruit

50 g (2 oz/generous ¼ cup) light brown soft sugar

10 mint leaves, finely chopped

Preheat the oven to 160°C (350°F/gas 4). Grease a 20 cm (8 inch) springform cake tin (pan) and line the base with baking parchment.

Put the butter into a saucepan over a medium heat and brown for 5–6 minutes until lovely brown specks appear. Transfer to a bowl to cool.

As it cools, muddle the pineapple. Combine all the ingredients in a bowl and set aside.

In a clean and dry bowl, whisk the aquafaba with the cream of tartar and salt for 3–4 minutes until frothy, then add the sugar and whisk for a further 4–5 minutes until you can form a ribbon from the whisk (we're not looking for stiff peaks here). Whisk in the cooled brown butter, milk, vanilla extract and almond extract.

Mix together the ground almonds, flour and baking powder and fold into the wet ingredients until combined. Pour the cake batter into the prepared tin, then spoon over the muddled pineapple, drizzling some of the minty syrup over.

Bake in the oven for 50–55 minutes until a skewer inserted into the centre comes out clean. Allow to cool completely before slicing.

COFFEE MISO CARAMEL CHOCOLATE PUDDING

SERVES 8   PREP TIME: 20 MINUTES   COOK TIME: 40 MINUTES

Miso and coffee are two of my favourite ingredients and they work so well together in a caramel sauce. This pudding is so comforting and comes together so quickly. This is the Sunday pud of all puds! It should be made during peak winter and served with a scoop of vegan vanilla ice cream.

50 g (2 oz) silken tofu

250 ml (8½ fl oz/1 cup) soya milk

1 tablespoon instant coffee granules

1 tablespoon boiling water

150 ml (5 fl oz/scant ⅔ cup) olive oil

150 g (5 oz/generous ¾ cup) light brown soft sugar

1 tablespoon vanilla extract

225 g (8 oz/1¾ cups) plain (all-purpose) flour

75 g (2½ oz/scant ⅔ cup) cocoa powder

2 teaspoons baking powder

1½ teaspoons bicarbonate of soda (baking soda)

½ teaspoon salt

non-dairy vanilla ice cream, to serve

FOR THE CARAMEL

95 g (3¼ oz/½ cup) light brown soft sugar

2 tablespoons white miso paste

2 tablespoons instant coffee granules

1 tablespoon vanilla extract

190 ml (6½ fl oz/generous ¾ cup) boiling water

Preheat the oven to 160°C (350°F/gas 4). Grease a 25 cm (10 inch) dish.

Blend the tofu and milk in a food processor, then set aside in a jug (pitcher). In a small cup, dissolve the coffee granules in the boiling water, then add to the jug along with the olive oil, brown sugar and vanilla extract. Whisk until combined.

Sift the flour, cocoa powder, baking powder, bicarbonate of soda and salt into a large bowl. Whisk to combine, then add the wet ingredients to the dry and fold in with a spatula.

Pour the batter into the dish and set aside.

To make the caramel, combine the sugar, miso paste, coffee and vanilla extract in a jug or bowl. Add the boiling water and stir to dissolve.

Pour the hot caramel mixture immediately over the batter. It will sink to the bottom and create a caramel sauce. Carefully place the dish into the oven and bake for 40 minutes.

Once the pudding is baked, allow it to sit for 10 minutes. Serve warm with vanilla ice cream.

ODE TO MANGOES

A lot of people think they love mangoes. But Jamaicans, like, really LOVE mangoes. We love them in a very special way that is hard to comprehend or put into words. A vast amount of mango trees grew in my garden in Jamaica, with the varying types ripening at different times in the year, and when they yield at their peak, it's one of the best things in the world. A perfectly ripe mango is my dream thing to eat.

What no one tells you about moving outside of a tropical country is how you'll spend most of your year yearning for a good mango and instead settling for a 'meh' mango. Whenever I go home, I eat as many as possible to make up for lost time. These recipes are best made during mango season and I've advised for the different types of mangos that are suitable for each one.

MANGO PISTACHIO LOAF WITH MANGO BUTTER

SERVES 6–8   PREP TIME : 30 MINUTES, PLUS 15 MINUTES SOAKING TIME   COOK TIME : 55 MINUTES

Although I didn't grow up eating Alphonso mangos in Jamaica, being based
in England now, my proximity to them via India is very good. They are creamy
and insanely fragrant. The flesh is tender and has a nectar-like quality that works
so perfectly when puréed and baked in a loaf cake. This recipe has two mango
elements, as I use dried mango for the mango butter. Dried mango
is addictive on it's own, but in this application it acts as the perfect
icing (frosting) for this nutty rich loaf.

100 g (3½ oz/⅔ cup) pistachios,
plus extra to decorate

250 g (9 oz/2 cups) plain
(all-purpose) flour

1½ teaspoons baking powder

½ teaspoon bicarbonate of soda
(baking soda)

½ teaspoon salt

200 g (7 oz) tinned mango slices in
syrup, drained and syrup reserved

150 g (5 oz/generous ¾ cup) light brown
soft sugar

1 tablespoon vanilla extract

100 g (3½ oz) plain non-dairy yoghurt

zest of 2 lemons

75 ml (2½ fl oz/5 tablespoons) olive oil

FOR THE MANGO BUTTER

100 g (3½ oz) dried mango

juice of 2 lemons

170 g (6 oz) room-temperature vegan
cream cheese

Preheat the oven to 160°C (350°F/gas 4). Grease
a 900 g (2 lb/9 x 5 x 3 inch) loaf tin (pan) and line with
baking parchment lengthways, with the parchment
lengthways, with the paper overhanging the ends of the
tin, so that the cake will be easy to remove once baked.

Start by making the mango butter. Put the dried mango
into a bowl and cover with boiling water. Leave to soak for
15 minutes until softened, then drain and blend in a food
processor with the lemon juice and cream cheese until
smooth. Transfer to a bowl and set aside while you make
the cake.

In a food processor, blend the pistachios to a powder.

Sift the flour, baking powder and bicarbonate of soda
into a bowl, then add to the pistachios and salt and
mix to combine.

Blend the flesh of the mangoes in a food processor until
completely smooth. Sieve it into a bowl to help remove
any extra fibres. Add the brown sugar, vanilla extract,
yoghurt, lemon zest and olive oil. Whisk until thoroughly
combined, then add the wet ingredients to the dry, folding
in with a spatula.

Pour the batter into the prepared tin and bake in the oven
for 50–55 minutes until a skewer inserted into the centre
comes out clean. Remove the cake from the oven and
leave to cool.

While the cake is cooling, pour 200 ml (7 fl oz/scant 1 cup)
of the syrup into a saucepan. Bring to the boil and allow
to reduce for 3–4 minutes. Set aside. Using a cocktail stick
(toothpick), pierce holes into the loaf. Pour the hot syrup
evenly over the cooling cake and allow to completely cool
in the tin before turning out. Slice into thick slices with
a serrated knife and serve with a dollop of the mango
butter and a scattering of pistachios.

BAKED MANGO CHEESECAKE

SERVES 6–8   PREP TIME : 25 MINUTES   COOK TIME : 1 HOUR 10 MINUTES

Cheesecake is one of those desserts that I don't often have, but when I do, I wonder why I don't. As much as I appreciate a no-bake cheesecake, I think baked cheesecake is my preferred form of sweet creamy cheese dessert. Apart from the classic vanilla baked cheesecake, I often go for something with citrus. The mango in this recipe really cuts through the richness, making it feel so much lighter. It also definitely tastes better the next day, so I recommend making it the day before to allow all the flavours to sit and develop.

300 g (10½ oz) Biscoff biscuits

100 g (3½ oz) vegan block butter, melted

2 Alphonso mangoes, peeled and flesh chopped (about 300 g/10½ oz flesh)

340 g (8½ oz) vegan cream cheese

100 g (3½ oz) silken tofu

juice and zest of 2 lemons

1 tablespoon vanilla

50 g (2 oz/generous ¼ cup) light brown soft sugar

3 tablespoons cornflour (cornstarch)

Preheat the oven to 160°C (350°F/gas 4). Grease a 20 cm (8 inch) springform cake tin (pan) and line the base with baking parchment.

In a food processor or using a ziplock bag and a rolling pan, blend or bash the biscuits into a powder. Transfer to a bowl, add the melted butter and mix with your hands. It should just come together when you squeeze it in your hands.

Place half of the biscuit base into the prepared tin and form the edge of the crust, then place the rest in the middle and form the base. Even it out using the bottom of a cup.

Bake in the oven for 10 minutes.

Meanwhile, make the filling by blending the flesh of the mangos in a food processor until smooth. Sieve it into a bowl to help remove any extra fibres. Put the cream cheese, tofu, lemon juice and zest and vanilla extract into the food processor and blend until smooth, then pour the mixture in with the mango. Finally, stir in the sugar and cornflour.

Remove the base from the oven and reduce the heat to 150°C (325°F/gas 3).

Pour the filling into the case and even out with a spatula. Place back in the oven to bake for 60 minutes, then turn the oven off and leave the cheesecake to cool completely in the oven.

You can serve this at room temperature or chill it first depending on when you're planning on eating it. I serve it on its own, but feel free to top with softly whipped vegan cream if desired.

BLACK PEPPER PAVLOVA WITH FRESH MANGO AND VANILLA CREAM

SERVES 6–8   PREP TIME : 30 MINUTES, PLUS COOLING TIME   COOK TIME : 1 HOUR 40 MINUTES

I adore black pepper in desserts. That punchy, fiery kick works so well in contrast with sugar. Pavlovas are the kind of dessert that can become too sickly sweet really quickly. In this rendition, the mangoes are used in their raw form, so try to let them ripen to peak sweetness. I'm so thankful to the person that accidentally first whipped aquafaba and probably freaked out. They truly deserve to be in the vegan hall of fame. On behalf of everyone in the vegan community, we are truly grateful. Although it takes longer to reach those glossy silky stiff peaks than egg whites, it is truly a modern-day miracle.

aquafaba from 1 x 400 g (14 oz) tin of chickpeas

¼ teaspoon salt

½ teaspoon cream of tartar

100 g (3½ oz/scant ½ cup) cane sugar

50 g (2 oz/generous ¼ cup) light brown soft sugar

¼ teaspoon xanthan gum

25 g (¾ oz/scant ¼ cup) cornflour (cornstarch)

1½ teaspoons freshly ground black pepper

FOR THE TOPPINGS

150 ml (5 fl oz/scant ⅔ cup) non-dairy whipping cream

2 tablespoons caster (superfine) sugar

1 vanilla pod (bean), seeds scraped out

3–4 ripe mangos, peeled and sliced

zest of 1 lime

toasted flaked (slivered) almonds, to decorate

Preheat the oven to 130°C (300°F/gas 2). Line two baking sheets with two 25 cm (10 inch) circles of baking parchment.

Pour the aquafaba into the bowl of a stand mixer, ensuring that it is totally clean and dry. This is important to make sure that the aquafaba whips. Whisk on a medium-high speed for 2–3 minutes until it begins to foam a little, then add the salt and cream of tartar. Whisk again for 2–3 minutes. Then, add the cane sugar and light brown soft sugar a tablespoon at a time, ensuring that each addition is fully incorporated before adding the next spoonful. Continue for 4–5 minutes until all the sugar is whisked in. Now add the xanthan gum and continue to whisk for 2 minutes more. The mixture should be glossy and stable. Add the cornflour a tablespoon at a time and then briefly whisk through the black pepper.

Using a spatula, divide the meringue mixture between the two circles of baking parchment, smoothing out the tops and adding some decorative peaks.

Bake in the oven for 20 minutes, then reduce the heat to 120°C (275°F/gas 1) and bake for 1 hour 20 minutes. more Turn off the oven and leave the meringues to cool completely in the oven without opening the door – you can do this overnight.

When the meringues have cooled, prepare the toppings. Whip the cream with the caster sugar. Once it has reached soft peaks, add the vanilla seeds and fold in. Divide the cream between the two meringes and top both with the sliced mangoes. Stack on top of each other and decorate with the lime zest and toasted flaked almonds.

PICKLE AND

CONDIMENT CITY

Pickles and condiments enhance most dishes. Added at the end of plating, they tend to round out the flavours in a dish. I love quickly pickled, thinly sliced red onions on a sandwich or a lunch bowl or a viciously pokey and flavoursome hot sauce on the top of a tofu scramble. These are my go-to recipes.

DIFFERENT WAYS TO USE JERK

Jerk is a cooking style native to Jamaica, using a jerk spice which is a combination of allspice and Scotch bonnets as the base. Traditionally, jerk is cooked over pimento wood, for that smoky flavour, and is normally meat-based. Jerk is so wonderfully versatile. I've included a few ways that you can incorporate it into your everyday cooking, through my classic jerk, fresh wet green jerk (which is more like a crossover between green seasoning and jerk) and then jerk butter, which is brilliant on vegetables and starchy vegetables.

DEE'S CLASSIC JERK SEASONING

1 onion, roughly chopped

8 garlic cloves

50 g (2 oz) fresh ginger root, peeled

1 tablespoon allspice berries

1 tablespoon coriander seeds

1–2 Scotch bonnets

2 tablespoons olive oil

65 ml (2½ fl oz/generous ¼ cup) soy sauce

zest and juice of 2 limes

1 tablespoon ground cinnamon

25 g (¾ oz) black treacle (molasses)

2 spring onions (scallions)

salt

Preheat the oven to 180°C (400°F/gas 6).

Put the onion, 6 of the garlic cloves, the ginger, allspice, coriander seeds and Scotch bonnet on a baking tray (pan). Toss with the olive oil and then season with sea salt. Roast in the oven for 40 minutes until everything is caramelised.

Transfer to a food processor with the soy sauce, remaining garlic, lime zest and juice, cinnamon, treacle and spring onions and blend until smooth.

Store in a clean jar and refrigerate for up to 2 weeks.

FRESH WET GREEN JERK

SERVES 8   PREP TIME : 5 MINUTES

bunch of coriander (cilantro)

bunch of flat-leaf parsley

4 spring onions (scallions)

1 Scotch bonnet

1 tablespoon allspice berries

1 teaspoon ground cinnamon

zest and juice of 4 limes

6 garlic cloves

2 tablespoons olive oil

2 teaspoons salt

In a food processor, blend all the ingredients into a paste. Store in a clean jar and refrigerate for up to 1 week.

JERK BUTTER

SERVES 4–5   MAKES 100 G (3½OZ)   PREP TIME : 5 MINUTES

100 g vegan block butter, softened

3 tablespoons Dee's Classic Jerk Seasoning (see page 205)

Mix together the softened butter and jerk seasoning until smooth, then refrigerate until needed.

GREEN SEASONING

SERVES 10–12   PREP TIME : 3 MINUTES

This flavour bomb is great to add to stews, soups and marinades.

bunch of coriander (cilantro)
bunch of flat-leaf parsley
10 springs of thyme, leaves picked
5 spring onions (scallions), roughly chopped
2 celery stalks, roughly chopped
1 bulb of garlic, cloves peeled
1 onion, roughly chopped
1 green (bell) pepper, roughly chopped
1 Scotch bonnet
sea salt and freshly ground black pepper

Put all the ingredients in a food processor and blend for 2–3 minutes to your desired consistency. I like mine quite fine, but you might like yours more coarse.

Store in a clean jar and refrigerate for up to 2 weeks.

MUSHROOM XO

SERVES 8–10   PREP TIME : 5 MINUTES   COOK TIME : 35 MINUTES

I adore mushrooms, particularly in their dried form. They add so much depth of flavour, and are even meatier than the fresh kind. I love to use this mushroom XO on toast with vegan butter, stirred into a noodle bowl, or on top of a freshly steamed rice bowl. This XO has so much flavour, and it has a big pay off in its versatility.

300 g (10½ oz) shallots, peeled and roughly chopped
8 garlic cloves, chopped
2 teaspoons chilli flakes
250 g (9 oz) dried shiitake mushrooms, soaked and chopped
1 nori sheet, shredded
125 ml (4 fl oz/½ cup) olive oil
3 tablespoons dark soy sauce
1½ teaspoons dark brown soft sugar
1½ teaspoons ground allspice
1 teaspoon salt

Blend the shallots in a food processor until smooth, then scrape out into a bowl and set aside. Put the garlic, chilli flakes, shiitake mushrooms and nori into the processor, blend, then set aside.

Heat the oil in a saucepan over a medium heat. Fry the shallots for 20 minutes, stirring frequently, until they look like soft caramel.

Add the mushroom mixture, cook for 10 minutes more, then add the soy sauce, sugar, allspice and salt. Cook for a further 3 minutes, then remove from the heat. Taste and adjust the seasoning if needed.

Store in a clean jar and refrigerate for up to 2 weeks.

SORREL HOISIN GLAZE

SERVES 3–4   PREP TIME : 5 MINUTES   COOK TIME : 10 MINUTES

Sorrel is a hibiscus drink. The floral notes really work with
the sweetness of the hoisin sauce. This would work well
in various dishes, especially anything crispy and fried.

400 ml (13 fl oz/generous 1½ cups) sorrel
soft drink

1 Scotch bonnet

4 allspice berries

100 ml (3/2 fl oz/scant ½ cup)
hoisin sauce

Combine the sorrel, whole Scotch bonnet and allspice
in a saucepan, bring to the boil, then reduce by half –
it should hold on the back of a spoon and be sticky.

Add the hoisin sauce, then transfer to a clean jar
and store for up to 2 weeks in the refrigerator.

SPICY PINEAPPLE JAM

SERVES 8–10   PREP TIME : 5 MINUTES   COOK TIME : 10 MINUTES

This jam is savoury! I'm a big fan of sweet and spicy
flavours – probably my favourite contrasting
combinations. My top tip would be to make
a grilled cheese using this jam.

1 small pineapple, peeled and chopped
(about 500 g/1 lb 2 oz flesh)

2 Scotch bonnets

4 garlic cloves

150 g (5 oz/generous ⅔ cup)
preserving sugar

50 g (2 oz/generous ¼ cup) light brown
soft sugar

Combine everything in a saucepan and bring to the boil,
then boil for 8 minutes. Reduce the heat, cover and
simmer for a further 45 minutes. Transfer to sterilised
jars (see page 223) and store for 3–4 weeks.

PICKLED CHO CHO

SERVES 8   PREP TIME: 5 MINUTES   COOK TIME: 5 MINUTES

400 ml (13 fl oz/generous 1½ cups) white wine vinegar

200 ml (7 fl oz/scant 1 cup) water

1 tablespoon allspice berries

1 tablespoon black peppercorns

1 tablespoon fennel seeds

2 tablespoons caster (superfine) sugar

3 chayote (cho cho), very finely sliced

2 cloves garlic

1 onion, sliced into half-moons

2 Scotch bonnets, finely sliced

In a saucepan, bring the vinegar and water to the boil. Add the allspice, peppercorns, fennels seeds and sugar to the pan and stir until the sugar has dissolved.

Add the remaining ingredients to a sterilised jar (see page 223) and pour the hot vinegar solution over it. Allow to cool completely, then transfer to the refrigerator and enjoy for up to 3 weeks.

CLASSIC JAMAICAN ESCOVITCH PICKLE

SERVES 8   PREP TIME: 5 MINUTES   COOK TIME: 5 MINUTES

Escovitch is normally served with fried fish, but this would be great on a sandwich! It's spicy and heady with allspice.

400 ml (13 fl oz/generous 1½ cups) white wine vinegar

200 ml (7 fl oz/scant 1 cup) water

1 tablespoon allspice berries

2 tablespoons caster (superfine) sugar

1 red (bell) pepper, finely sliced

1 yellow (bell) pepper, finely sliced

1 orange (bell) pepper, finely sliced

2 cloves garlic

1 onion, sliced into half-moons

2 Scotch bonnets, finely sliced

In a saucepan, bring the vinegar and water to the boil. Add the allspice and sugar to the pan and stir until the sugar has dissolved.

Add the remaining ingredients to a sterilised jar (see page 223) and pour the hot vinegar solution over it. Allow to cool completely, then transfer to the refrigerator and enjoy for up to 3 weeks.

GLOSSARY

ACKEE

Ackee is a fruit from the same family as the lychee and longan, though it is eaten mostly in savoury dishes, like a vegetable. It's silky and creamy, with a very unique flavour that is unlike any other ingredient you'll ever try. Ackee is a staple in Jamaican cooking, the tree bearing fruit all year round, and forms part of our national dish, ackee and salt fish. I love using ackee to make mayonnaise and creamy sauces, otherwise I like to eat it very traditionally with rice or fried dumplings.

AQUAFABA

Aquafaba is the often discarded liquid from tinned chickpeas, which is used as an egg white replacement in vegan baking. Whipping up stiff, glossy peaks of aquafaba still seems to me like an amazing magic trick – I feel like a magician and surprise myself every time. I love using it in cakes and for pavlova.

BAMMY

Bammy is a type of gluten-free bread made with cassava. It can be fried or steamed, and it's typically served with fish. I love fried bammy the most, as when it's cooked to perfection, it's chewy, crispy and salty.

BROWNING

Browning is a sauce made from burnt or caramelised sugar that is used as the base for various Jamaican dishes and marinades to add depth in flavour.

CALLALOO

Callaloo, otherwise known as amaranth, is a wonderful dark leafy green that is so earthy and grounding. This is the green that I grew up eating the most, and I've found I love it more the older I've become. I love eating callaloo fried and steamed with lots of garlic and frazzled onions.

CHO CHO

Cho cho (chayote) is a wonderful vegetable with a flavour and texture that is a cross between celery and cucumber. It's so delicious eaten raw, when its crisp and refreshing qualities can shine. I enjoy pickling them and eating them in burger or sandos.

ESCOVITCH

Escovitch is a spicy, vinegary pickle that consists of (bell) peppers, onions, spring onions (scallions), Scotch bonnets and seasoning. Escovitch is best served with fried food, where it cuts through the richness.

HARD DOUGH BREAD

Hard dough bread is a dense and slightly sweet buttery bread. Fresh hard dough bread from Captain's Bakery in Jamaica was a huge part of my childhood. It's so good you can eat it on its own.

HARD FOOD

Hard food refers to ground provisions such as boiled yam, plantain, potato, sweet potato and dumplings. This is used as a side, to be served with main dishes. I particularly love brown stew with hard food.

NOOCH

Nutritional yeast, or nooch, adds a wonderfully umami/nutty flavour to dishes. I love using it in seasonings or when making cheesy or creamy sauces.

PATTY

Patties are the main fast food in Jamaica – if you are out on the road shopping or running errands, a patty is the go-to thing to eat. The most traditional filling is beef, but I always loved them with cheese as a kid, which is why I wrote a recipe for one for the book (see pages 106–10).

PIMENTO

Pimento is another name for allspice, which is the spice used as the base for a lot of Jamaican dishes, including jerk. The berries grow on a tree and have a beautiful smoky flavour. I adore pimento and love using in spice blends when roasting squash and other veg.

ROTI

A type of flatnread native to the Indian subcontinent and popular in Jamaica. Flaky roti is one of my favourite things to eat in the world. I have time and space for all kinds of roti – I love them in all their forms. For me, a roti is best enjoyed with a curry, with tamarind sauce on the side.

RUNDOWN

Rundown is a light coconut sauce that includes the Jamaican Holy Trinity of thyme, spring onion (scallion) and Scotch bonnet. Traditionally, rundown tends to be made with salted and cured mackerel, but I love using cured artichokes, which add that briny flavour.

SCOTCH BONNET

Scotch bonnets are my favourite chilli – fruity, floral and wickedly spicy. I adore their recognisable scent when cooked whole in a pot of rice and peas, and their intense heat in a jerk marinade or rub.

SORREL

Sorrel is fruity, spiced drink normally made during Christmas and spiked with a lot of white rum. The main ingredient in sorrel is hibiscus, which on its own is tart and therefore perfect for making a sticky and tangy glaze! My mum often uses the hibiscus flowers from her sorrel to make jams (jellies) and chutneys. It's such a wonderful, unique flavour.

SPINNERS

Spinners are dumplings made with a simple dough of water and flour that are added to soups, stews and curries. They soak up all the flavour of whatever you cooked them with, and are always my favourite bit to eat. There's nothing more annoying that buying a Jamaican soup and not getting a respectable amount of spinners.

TOSTONES

Tostones are pressed, fried green plantains. Unlike sweet, ripe plantain, green plantain is a lot more fibrous and starchy. I adore eating fried green plantain with a spicy, savoury dip or ceviche-like dish.

ABOUT THE AUTHOR

Denai Moore is an acclaimed British-Jamaican musician turned chef. Denai's pop-up, Dee's Table, has received praise from *Metro*, *Vice* and *Dojo*, and was featured on Jamie Oliver's television series *Jamie's Meat-Free Meals*. As a recipe developer, Denai has written for the *Guardian*, and has held cooking demonstrations for *Time Out*. In 2022, she was named one of Forbes 30 Under 30. Denai predominately cooks from a place of nostalgia, combining her food memories with her love of international cuisines. Her unique cooking style speaks to a new generation of home cooks, culinary rule breakers and restaurant goers, as well as to those reconnecting with their roots in a new way.

THANK YOU

This feels really hard to write; there are so many amazing people that helped me along in the journey to Plentiful. I'll try to keep it short and sweet and hope that if I forget anyone, I can make it up to them by bringing them some passion fruit doughnuts!

TO KAJAL AND THE HARDIE GRANT TEAM: thank you for allowing me to make the book of my dreams! This book literally wouldn't be possible without you. When I wrote my proposal in 2019, I couldn't have wished for a better home to publish it.

TO SILE: thank you for being so understanding, for welcoming the world of Plentiful and validating me along the way. Thank you for being patient with me as I made countless amendments to the proposal. It's strange to think how much it has evolved.

TO LUCY: my editing queen! Thank you for your patience, for understanding my very off-script book ideas and for making my own words make more sense. This process was so much easier with you!

TO MY FAMILY: thank you for affirming me over the years as I embarked on this ever-changing Dee's Table journey. From my first supper club at 10 Cable Street to countless late markets, thank you for your help when I was short-staffed and for driving me before I could drive myself.

TO NADIRA: thank you so much for encouraging me as I pushed past the author imposter syndrome, and for helping me when I wrote the proposal – you made it look a lot sleeker than my Microsoft Paint-esque design skills would have allowed!

TO YUKI: thank you for capturing the recipes so well! For inviting the whole Plentiful team into your studio and having a killer music playlist that nestled us into place as we worked in a heatwave!

TO RACHEL: thank you for your incredible taste in cookware and tables. I've been trying to source a great red table since the shoot.

TO NANCY: thank you for your beautiful ceramics and bowls, I've captured so many Dee's Table recipes using your wonderful pieces, that it only felt right for you to be a part of this book.

TO ALBION STORES: thank you for styling me for this book. The pieces you lent me really helped to tie everything together.

TO CHRISTINA: thank you so much for blessing *Plentiful* with your beautiful gaze. My favourite thing about Jamaica is how rich and green it is. You capture nature in the best of ways!

TO JOSS AND HATTIE: thank you for making my food look so good! I loved watching you both cook through my recipes, affirming to me that I wasn't insane. I was somehow terrified that all the recipes would go horribly wrong (deep in my pre-first day shoot nerves) but they instantly went away after the first two recipes.

TO EVI-O.STUDIO AND KAIT: thank you for making my book look so good! I really wanted to create a fun yet inviting cookbook, and this is beyond my Pinterest dreams.

TO ROB: thank you for being such a supportive friend and offering your wonderful home to shoot the Margate portion of the book. Your garden was the perfect backdrop for my favourite shot in the book – an ode to mangoes!

TO NEELA, SUHAIYLA, JON KEY, JAR KEY: thank you for being such beautiful guests and looking insanely stunning in my shoot!? It was so lovely to have the warmth of amazing friends be a part of this journey, to make the book just a little more special.

CURVE STOREROOM: thank you for providing such a wonderful and peaceful space to edit in. I sat in your café for an embarrassing amount of time, probably even more than my own home. Your vegan Rueben sando, banana bread and amazing oat flat whites kept me going as I tried to utilise the full force of my final three brain cells post-pandemic.

THANK YOU TO EVERYONE that tasted all my early tests and provided crucial feedback when I had become too close to the recipes and the book.

FINALLY THANK YOU, YOU! The reader, reading this. If the book caught your eye and we're just meeting for the first time on this page, if you've followed Dee's Table for years, if you've eaten my food at a supper club or Parisian festival, or if you've made one of my recipes and shared it with someone you love (including yourself). Thank you for your support.

I hope you enjoy Plentiful and it can live happily on your shelf for years to come.

COOK'S NOTES

All fruits and vegetables are assumed to be medium-sized and washed. Garlic, onions and ginger are assumed to be peeled.

Herbs are assumed to be fresh unless stated otherwise.

Salt is assumed to be fine sea salt unless stated otherwise.

All oven temperatures are for fan ovens – please adjust accordingly if using a standard non-fan oven.

Tablespoon and teaspoon measurements given are level.
1 teaspoon = 5 ml / 1 tablespoon = 15 ml.

To sterilise a jar for storing preserves, wash in warm soapy water, then transfer to an oven preheated to 160°C (350°F/gas 4) to dry out.

Published in 2023 by Hardie Grant Books,
an imprint of Hardie Grant Publishing

Hardie Grant Books (London)
5th & 6th Floors
52–54 Southwark Street
London SE1 1UN

Hardie Grant Books (Melbourne)
Building 1, 658 Church Street
Richmond, Victoria 3121

hardiegrantbooks.com

British Library Cataloguing-in-Publication Data. A catalogue record for this book
is available from the British Library.

Plentiful
ISBN: 978-178488-549-6

10 9 8 7 6 5 4 3 2 1

Publishing Director: Kajal Mistry
Editor: Lucy Kingett
Proofreader: Theresa Bebbington
Photographer: Yuki Sugiura
Design: Evi-O.Studio | Kait Polkinghorne
Prop Stylist: Rachel Vere
Food Stylist: Joss Herd
Food Styling Assistant: Hattie Arnold
Production Controller: Sabeena Atchia

Colour reproduction by p2d
Printed and bound in China by Leo Paper Products Ltd.